36 Best Christmas Party Ideas

36 BEST Christmas Party Ideas

by MARTY SPRAGUE

THE SUMMIT GROUP • FORT WORTH, TEXAS

THE SUMMIT GROUP
1227 West Magnolia, Suite 500 • Fort Worth, Texas 76104

99 98 97 96 95 94   5 4 3 2 1

Library of Congress Cataloging-in-Publication

Sprague, Marty, 1949-
36 best Christmas Party ideas / Marty Sprague.
p. cm.
Includes bibliographical references.
ISBN 1-56530-142-0: $12.95
1. Entertaining. 2. Christmas. I. Title. II. Title: Thirty-six best Christmas party ideas.
GV1472.7.C5S67 1994
793.2'2—dc20   94-24424
CIP

Cover and book design by David Sims
Illustrated by Greg King

To my wonderful husband, Brad, and our three precious children, Amy, Chris, and Abby—thank you for all the sacrifices you've made to allow me to write.
You are always the loves of my life.

And thank you to the King of Christmas, Jesus Christ, the Lord of my life.

Glory to God in the highest, and on earth peace to men on whom His favor rests.
LUKE 2:14

Table of Contents

Which Party Is for You?

	Couples Party	Office Party	Singles Party	Women Only Party	Family Party	Reach-out or Benefit
Christmas Express Party	X	X	X			X
White Elephant Christmas Party	X	X	X	X	X	
"The Twelve Days of Christmas" Party	X	X	X		X	
Tales of Christmas Party	X	X	X	X	X	
Little Christmas Eve Party	X		X	X	X	
Chestnuts Roasting on an Open Fire Party	X	X	X			
Share the Joy of Christmas Party	X	X	X			X
Christmas Caroling Progressive Party	X		X		X	
Sounds of Christmas Party	X	X	X		X	X
A Christmas Carol Party	X	X	X			
Love Wrap Party	X		X	X	X	X
He Is the Reason for the Season Party	X		X	X	X	
It's a Wonderful Life! Party	X	X	X		X	
Latino Christmas Celebration	X	X	X			
Christmas Midnight Buffet	X	X	X			
Not Another Christmas Banquet! Party	X	X	X	X		X
Chinese Christmas Party	X	X	X			
It's Time to Decorate Your House Party	X	X	X	X	X	

	Couples Party	Office Party	Singles Party	Women Only Party	Family Party	Reach-out or Benefit
Hats off to Christmas! Party	X		X			X
Trim the Tree Party	X		X		X	X
Frosty's Favorite Christmas Party			X			X
Christmas Around the World Party	X		X			X
Christmas Can Be Nutty! Party	X	X	X	X	X	
Christmas Caroling Hayride	X	X	X		X	
Semiformal Christmas Dinner Party		X	X			
Ladies Night Out Christmas Party		X		X		
Christmas Cookie Decorating Party			X	X		
Christmas Brunch and Ornament Exchange		X		X		
Santa's Workshop Party				X		
Christmas Friendship Party		X		X		
Christmas Tea Party		X				
Christmas Craft and Dessert Party		X		X		
Great Cookie Swap				X		
Baskets of Joy				X		X
Open House for Seniors	X		X	X	X	X
Cajun Christmas Feast	X		X	X	X	

Acknowledgments

To all those dear friends who so generously shared their hearts, their ideas, and their time so that you can plan the best Christmas parties ever. Thank you all so much! I appreciate you more than you can imagine.

Donna Aigner
Nancy Asnon
Brenda Barnett
Sandra Barnett
Patti Beckman
Woody Beckman
Phyllis Bell
Ursula Belzer
Beverly Brandon
Kim Brandt
Carol and Lona Brown
H. Jackson Brown, Jr.
Lisa Brown
Rosemary Brown
Lisa Bue
Jeff and Melanie Bufkin
Harold Bullock
Katy Byerts
Kim Casazza
Donna Christian
Darla Coker
Claire Collins
Barbara Cook
Connie Courtney
Holly Demetrescu

Mary DiRienzo
Judy Dodd
Ruth Early
Marsha Evancoe
Suzanne Frank
Mindy and Seth Gatchell
Debbie Hall
Jan Hayes
Polly Hernandez
Carol Howard
Katie Humphreys
Julie Kassouf
Cindy Ketner
Kathy King
Kathy Kruip
C. W. Lambert
Susan Lavelle
Sue Love
Joan Massey
Denna Mayer
Mary Anne McGlynn
Sallie Meinen
Ruth Miller
Charlotte Mueller
Dorraine and Cruise Palmer

Karen Palmer
Sara Pecina
Beverly Petersen
Melony Puz
Laura Quay
Kathy Rust
Rod and Debbie Sanders
Mary Sterling
Judy Steyer
Wanda Strappazon
Karen Tang
Elizabeth Thomas
Tim Thomas
Becky Unrau
Becky Vorster
Carol Walter
Donna Warren
Kay and Rick Warren
Jan Webb
Candy Williams
Denise Williams
Lindy Wilson
Jane Witt
Madeleine Wolfe
Anne Wolfer

Introduction

This is a book about fun: wild, crazy, out-of-the-ordinary Christmas fun.

Last year my friend Mark wanted to throw a terrific holiday celebration. So he went to every bookstore in town to get some party ideas. But he couldn't find a thing—not one book to help him plan a special Christmas party. *36 Best Christmas Party Ideas* was written for people like Mark, and people like you, who want to plan a creative and memorable party, tailor-made for you and your friends.

It is written as an idea springboard for:

- Couples who are tired of the same old Christmas potluck supper they've attended for the past twenty-seven years.

- Men and women desperate for a creative and exciting office party.

- Singles who are looking for a way to have a roaring, good time, and also do something beneficial for others.

- Ladies who want to go to a fabulous Christmas party, not just cook for one!

Look carefully at the chart entitled "Which Party Is for You?" Then choose one that is just right, and start planning your celebration!

Keep in mind that we are not trying to stifle your creativity! For those who need step-by-step details, here they are. But for those who like to run with your own ideas, great. Just use our suggestions to spur you on to bigger and better parties. Face it: you may still have to attend a few boring Christmas parties in the future, but you'll never have to host one like that again!

As you plan any of the Christmas parties in this book, remember several important party principles:

- Invite more people than your room will accommodate. As long as you have enough food and enough chairs, "too many people" almost always equals "just the right number"!

- Send out your invitations early—four to six weeks before the event. Don't let everyone else plan their party before you do; yours is going to be terrific this year!

- Complete every possible task for your party ahead of time so that you can enjoy your guests—not spend your whole evening in the kitchen.

- After the guests arrive, be flexible, and learn to laugh at the unexpected. If someone spills red fruit punch on your white rug, or your cat scales the buffet table to enjoy the shrimp dip, relax! Little calamities will only ruin the party if you let them. Your guests will be having such a fabulous time that they may not even notice!

Christmas is truly a season of joy "for those who have eyes to see and ears to hear." I hope this book will help you and your loved ones experience that joy as you plan wonderful Christmas parties. And further, I pray that you will experience His great love that came down the first Christmas...

God bless you!
MARTY SPRAGUE

Top Ten Reasons You Know Your Christmas Party Will Bomb:

No. 10
You hired nonunion elves.

No. 9
Your fruitcake isn't high fiber.

No. 8
You're serving a main course called "Filet of Rudolph!"

No. 7
Your gingerbread houses were condemned by Bob Vila.

No. 6
You've posted a sexual harassment policy notice next to the mistletoe.

No. 5
You saw your high-priced caterer sneaking out the back door of Jack-In-The-Box.

No. 4
Your take-home wreaths are made out of poison oak.

No. 3
The Environmental Protection Agency condemned last year's eggnog as toxic waste.

No. 2
You just saw your guest list featured on "America's Most Wanted" television show.

But the No. 1 reason you know your Christmas party will be a bomb:
You failed to read this book first!

Chapter 1

Christmas Express Party: Deck the Diesel

This party is the ideal way to honor employees and entertain friends while everyone experiences the joy of giving to a group of children in need. The Christmas Express—aboard a charter bus or trolley—pulls out all the stops.

Instruct everyone to dress in festive attire (and if your climate demands, warm coats for caroling) and meet at your home where the Christmas Express awaits. Then, the fun starts, packing as many entertaining activities as possible into one evening.

You might follow the lead of the meticulously planned route you've seen others choose. At the first destination of such a recent party, the Christmas Express group caroled at another couple's Christmas party. Their second stop was at a local orphanage where they visited with the children and gave each a specially chosen gift. (See Special Activities for more about this important element of the party.) They went on to the host's favorite restaurant for a festive meal. After dinner, guests hopped aboard the Christmas Express to compete in a Polaroid scavenger hunt. To top off the evening, the Christmas Express made a tour of

1

selected neighborhoods—and went to the city zoo—for a look at the beautiful Christmas lights and decorations.

Invitation Ideas

"We Invite You to Get On Board the Christmas Express!" tells your guests something special is in store. If your budget can afford custom invitations, have some printed with a bus or trolley pictured. If your printer suggests one in the shape of a bus or trolley, go for it if you can handle the extra one hundred dollars a die-cut adds to your printing bill. Inside, in addition to the date, time, attire, and where to meet for the evening, request an R.S.V.P. and provide your telephone number.

If your budget won't spring for custom printing, preprinted fill-in-the-blanks Christmas invitations are just fine. And they have the advantage of being quite a bit less expensive! Whichever you choose, slip in a card with information about the specific wrapped gift each guest should bring for a child. (See Special Activities for complete information.)

Setting the Mood

Decorations: If the charter company allows, put up a festive wreath and some small decorations or greenery at the front of the bus to welcome guests and make the occasion more festive.

Music: Ask the charter company if you can use the public address system on the bus to play Christmas music (learn whether it takes cassettes or compact discs). Or, if you know a skilled guitarist, ask him or her to lead the singing. Pass out copies of song sheets so everyone can sing along.

Enhancements: Before dark, gather all the guests together and take a group picture by the side of the bus—or take one indoors at the scavenger hunt. Once the photo is developed, have an enlargement made and mail copies to guests.

Special Activities

The evening's route and activities are open to your interpretation. Making a stop at an orphanage or shelter for children really adds to the Christmas spirit of unselfish giving, however. Call the orphanage or shelter before you send out invitations. Ask for a list of specific gifts your guests can bring for the children. Get names and ages if possible.

Choose a restaurant which can seat all your guests together in one room. If your party can be seated apart from other clientele, it will enhance the spirit of camaraderie. Like other locations to be visited, check out ahead of time for availability and find out if the parking will accommodate your Christmas Express bus.

A Polaroid scavenger hunt at a local mall can be a truly hilarious experience. This scavenger hunt involves a list of items of which participants take photographs. For example, one entry might read: "Find the Christmas tree with the burnt-out blue bulb and take a picture of it." Or, "Take a picture of the Salvation Army bell ringer with the red beard."

Theme Variations

Add to or delete any of the suggested activities. For example, delete caroling at another Christmas party and simply sing on the bus. Or, add dessert and coffee at the host's home at the end of the evening. For an entirely different Christmas Express, charter the bus for a half- or full-day trip to a mountain cabin or holiday resort approximately one to two hours' drive away.

Limitations and Logistics

Finances may be the biggest limitation for this party, so consider cohosting the evening with several other couples. If restaurant dining makes the cost of the party prohibitive, provide festive box suppers to be eaten en route.

Twenty-five to fifty people—or as many guests as the charter bus accommodates—is ideal for this party. Look for a bus that is well maintained, with comfortable seats. (One equipped with a washroom in the back is ideal.) Check to see if the bus is equipped with a microphone, so the host can emcee the evening. If you're in a city with trolleys available, consider chartering one.

Because careful attention to detail ensures a well-coordinated evening, one person should plan all activities and stops. Several people can help with the details—which should be taken care of far in advance, then double-checked a day or two before the party. Details (where applicable) include:

☞ **Charter vehicle:** Start by checking companies for competitive prices. Once you've chosen one, ask about regulations for groups, a seating plan for the bus, use of the bus sound system, and availability of a microphone.

☞ **Restaurant:** Make reservations at least one month or more ahead of time. Decide on menu. Check decor and seating, and make arrangements for payment of the bill. If you wish, give guests a choice of several entrees (beef, chicken, or seafood, for example) as well as a beverage, with the rest of the courses consistent.

   If box suppers are to be served, select foods that can be eaten at virtually any temperature. Make arrangements with a caterer well ahead of time, again checking companies for competitive prices.

☞ **Arrival and gift distribution time at the orphanage** as well as any pertinent rules.

☞ **Arrival time at the Christmas party where you are caroling** and any necessary arrangements with the host/hostess.

☞ **Planning the scavenger hunt** (including scouting out things to be photographed), securing Polaroid cameras, and determining arrival and departure times at the mall. (Be sure closing time is noted.)

☛ **Plan the specific route to view the best displays of lights and decorations.** If you plan to go into the zoo or some other public venue, be sure to note closing times.

☛ **Emcee:** The most outgoing, jovial host, hostess, or guest should act as emcee for the evening, leading caroling practice, telling funny stories, and keeping guests informed about details and directions for the next activity. This person is important to the evening's fun, but will also keep things running smoothly.

When some guests R.S.V.P., they may indicate that they can participate in only a portion of the festivities. Duplicate a simple map with approximate times for each destination and mail it to those guests. For everyone else, retain the element of surprise concerning your itinerary.

Randy and Sallie Meinen of Fort Worth, Texas, provided all the details for the Christmas Express Party.

Chapter 2

White Elephant Christmas Party

I f you're someone who loves giving parties where hilarity is the theme, try this special gathering. One couple's White Elephant party has become so popular over the years that they've had to move the festivities from their home to a nearby clubhouse to accommodate about sixty guests.

Old friends and new will experience the wilder, crazier side of Christmas when everyone learns someone else's interpretation of a White Elephant gift. In addition to a beautifully wrapped package—"something that no one would want"—ask each guest or couple to bring a Christmas snack or dessert. You'll provide the beverages, the party space, and your own White Elephant.

Invitation Ideas

Be creative! Find an elephant stamp and make a border of elephants, then run off your flyer on bright red or green paper. In addition to the usual who, what, when, where, why, your phone number for more details, and to R.S.V.P., instruct guests to bring a wrapped gift—provided that it's ugly, funny, or useless. Specify one gift per person or one per couple, and ask guests to bring a festive hors d'oeuvre or dessert that works well as a finger food. These invitations can be easily folded, stapled, stamped, and mailed—no envelope is necessary. (Informal preprinted Christmas invitations are also fine, especially for a small group.)

Setting the Mood

Decoration: The Christmas tree is the focal point of the evening, so make it striking—whether it's live or artificial, your own tree or one provided by the rented facility. Add some white elephants made from plastic or cardboard to the usual profusion of colorful ornaments on the tree, and march them among fresh garlands of greenery and other traditional decorations to make a festive serving table.

Music: Christmas music, popular and traditional, is a perfect background. (So that everyone can hear well during the gift exchange, consider turning off the music.)

Enhancements: Because many guests may not have met one another, name tags are a must at any potentially large gathering. Trace elephants from a pattern and cut them out of white card stock or construction paper. Upon arrival, guests can write their names on the elephants with red or green marker.

Depending upon your guest list, invitations might include a gentle reminder that crude or X-rated gifts are not appropriate. Ridiculous gadgets, hopelessly outdated items, and absolutely useless gifts such as a "genuine mink bellybutton warmer" get the biggest laughs.

Provide large trash cans for guests who wish to leave their "treasures" behind. Donate the remains to a charity thrift shop; most are able to sell anything and everything.

Special Activities

As guests arrive, have each draw a number and place his or her gift under the Christmas tree. Give everyone thirty to forty-five minutes to socialize and enjoy punch and snacks. Then, have guests choose a chair around the Christmas tree.

If you don't wish to do it yourself, preassign a fun, outgoing person to act as emcee and coordinator of the gift exchange, the primary activity. The emcee explains the gift exchange briefly and clearly:

1. One at a time, in numerical order, guests approach the tree, choose a gift, and unwrap it in front of the group.

2. After the first gift is opened, at his or her turn any guest can "steal" an already opened gift from another or choose an unopened gift from under the tree. Gifts cannot be opened before making the choice between stealing an opened gift or taking an unopened gift!

3. A gift can be stolen no more than three times after it is first opened. Thereafter, that gift is secure with its final owner and cannot be stolen again.

4. *Optional:* The guest who opened the first package can make one final steal at the very end of the exchange.

Theme Variations

At one White Elephant party I heard about, guests opened their gifts while sitting on Santa's knee!

Limitations and Logistics

Anywhere from twelve to sixty is an ideal number of guests, depending upon the size of the party room. The room should be large enough to accommodate not only a Christmas tree—big enough to place all the gifts under—but also a chair for each guest.

The atmosphere should be warm and inviting, with a roaring fire, for example. Set up one or more large tables for buffet-style service from all sides. Provide punch, hot cider, and coffee with guests' favorite festive treats. To save cleanup time, use holiday-decorated disposable paper goods and plastic ware.

Some preparty details:

☛ If you rent a facility, include money in your budget to cover the required deposit or room rental. To secure your ideal calendar date, make reservations for a party room three to six months in advance.

☛ Send out invitations four to six weeks in advance.

☛ Cut slips of paper, one per guest (the approximate number of expected guests plus last-minute extras), and number them. Put them in a fish bowl or colorful Christmas basket.

White Elephant Party is ideal for couples, singles, and as an office party.
Seth and Mindy Gatchell, of Irvine, California, introduced me to the White Elephant Party.

Chapter 3

"The Twelve Days of Christmas" Party

Young people like this concept—making a tradition of an annual Christmas party for neighborhoods, old and new. Invite current neighbors and also include friends from your old neighborhood—introducing the two by means of a holiday game party. It welcomes in the Christmas season with a spirit of friendship and laughter.

Invitation Ideas

Invitations can be simple red or green sheets run through a copier. Or, shop for preprinted ones that read "Neighborhood Open House." In addition to your name, the date, time, and location of the party, ask guests to "bring a dish for eight" and encourage them to "wear a Christmas sweater"—or hat or whatever—to the party. Add your telephone number and an R.S.V.P. if you wish.

Setting the Mood

Decorations: If you've decorated for the holidays early, you'll be all set. Stay with "The Twelve Days of Christmas" theme and

11

decorate the serving table simply with greenery, glowing candles, and pears piled into rustic baskets.

Music: Play Christmas music in the background during part of the evening, making sure "The Twelve Days of Christmas" is part of the musical mix. When guests "make their own music," turn off the CD or cassette player.

Enhancements: Build a fire. Keep potpourri simmering or wassail brewing to give off pleasing Christmas aromas. Add a gift exchange, perhaps with a theme such as gifts depicting "The Twelve Days of Christmas," gifts under one dollar, Christmas mugs, stocking stuffers, or thrift-store Christmas attire. Or, have guests bring board games, if they wish.

Special Activities

After everyone eats, set the tone for the fun ahead with a reading of "The Twelve Days of Christmas." (Go to the end of this chapter for text.)

Another "must" activity for this party: guests compose their own rendition of "The Twelve Days of Christmas." Divide up into teams—a great way to help people get to know one another better—and assign each "day," one through twelve. Each team must come up with original words for their assigned day—but related to being neighbors or living in their neighborhood. Encourage humor! For example, instead of "a partridge in a pear tree," substitute "a trash can without any lid."

Write each team's new line on a large poster board or blackboard. Then, before singing the new lyrics, designate certain groups—only men, all those who have small children, and so on—to sing certain "days," mixing groups for each verse. Everyone joins in on the final verse. By the end, guests should be out of breath, laughing, and totally at ease!

Break for refreshments, then those who wish to can move on to play games such as Pictionary—but using only Christmas words and themes. Or organize an amateur talent show with a Christmas theme. You may wish to end the evening with carols.

Theme Variations

To encourage guest participation, ask everyone to bring a snack, dessert, or dinner course appropriate to the party theme.

Limitations and Logistics

This party's only real limitation is the size of your home. If your living room or family room is small and comfortable for only eight or ten people, keep the party flowing through adjoining rooms. Rearrange sofas and chairs in the largest living area so guests can sit in a large circle. In a casual atmosphere such as this, the phrase "the more the merrier" takes on real meaning.

Name tags encourage conversation between those who haven't met one another.
Cut tags from construction paper or card stock to look like a pear (as in "a partridge in…") or another item in the song.

"The Twelve Days of Christmas" Party is ideal for couples, singles, families, or as an office party.
James and Claire Collins, formerly of Austin, Texas, first introduced me to "The Twelve Days of Christmas" concept.

"The Twelve Days of Christmas": A Reading

December 14
From:
Miss Agnes Gilstrap
3495 Copeland Drive
Anaheim, California 92816

Dearest Alfred,
I went to the door today when the postman delivered a partridge in a pear tree. What a thoroughly delightful gift. I couldn't have been more surprised or pleased.

> With deepest love and devotion,
> *Agnes*

December 15
My dearest Alfred,
Today the postman brought your very special and sweet gift. Just imagine my surprise at receiving two turtle doves. You're so thoughtful. They are adorable.

> All my love,
> *Agnes*

December 16
My dear Alfred,
Aren't you the extravagant one! Now, I really must protest. I do not deserve such generosity—three French hens! They are just darling, but I must insist, you have been too kind.

> Love,
> *Agnes*

December 17
My dear Alfred,
Today the postman delivered four calling birds. Now really, they are beautiful, but don't you think enough is enough? You're being too romantic.

> Affectionately,
> *Agnes*

December 18

Dear Alfred,

What a surprise! Today the postman delivered five golden rings—one for every finger. You're just impossible, but I do love the rings. Frankly, all those squealing birds are beginning to get on my nerves.

Gratefully,

Agnes

December 19

Dear Alfred,

When I opened the door, there were actually six geese-a-laying on my front steps. So, you're back to the birds again, huh? Those geese are huge! Where will I ever keep them? The neighbors are complaining, and I cannot sleep through the racket. PLEASE STOP!!!

Cordially,

Agnes

December 20

Alfred,

What's with you and all those birds? Seven swans-a-swimming! What kind of a joke is this? There are bird droppings all over the house, and I'm a nervous wreck! This is not funny, so STOP IT!!!

Sincerely,

Agnes

December 21

Alfred,

I think I prefer the birds! What do you expect me to do with eight maids-a-milking? As if it is not enough with all those birds, the eight maids-a-milking brought along their cows! There is manure all over the lawn, and I can't even move in my own house. Just lay off me, buddy!

Agnes

December 22

Hey, Smart Aleck!

What are you—some kind of sadist? Now there are nine pipers piping. And do they ever play! They haven't stopped chasing those maids since they got here. The cows are getting upset and are stepping all over those screeching birds. What am I going to do? The neighbors have started a petition to evict me!

You'll get yours!

Agnes

December 23

O.K., Buster!

Now there are ten ladies dancing! But I don't know why they're called ladies; they have been flirting with those pipers so much that the cows cannot sleep and have developed diarrhea. My living room is a pigsty! The Public Housing Authorities have subpoenaed me to show cause why my house should not be condemned. I'm going to sic the police on you, squirt!

One who means it,

Agnes

December 24

Listen, Dummy!

What's with these eleven lords dressed in tights, leaping and jumping like they've got Mexican jumping beans in their pants? Not only that, but they are about to drive those little maids crazy. All twenty-three birds are dead! I hope you are satisfied, you rotten, vicious swine!

Your sworn enemy,
Agnes

December 25

Law Offices of
Dewey, Cheatham, and Howe
303 Main Street
Los Angeles, California 90164
Dear Sir:

This is to acknowledge your latest gift of the twelve fiddlers fiddling, which you have seen fit to inflict on our client, Miss Agnes Gilstrap. The destruction, of course, was total. All future correspondence with her should come to our attention. Should you attempt to visit Miss Gilstrap at the Sunny Dale Sanitarium, the attendants have instructions to shoot you on sight.

Sincerely,
Dewey, Cheatham, and Howe

Chapter 4

Tales of Christmas Party

This party provides an elegant, traditional approach to Christmas. Guests socialize, partake of a magnificent catered dinner, and enjoy wonderful stories of Christmas recounted by a skilled storyteller—all in a lovely Victorian setting.

If you'd like to share your love of literature with friends, this party will remind them not only of Christmas tales by great authors, but also of times past. To make the ambiance complete, ask guests to come in costumes from the nineteenth or early twentieth century.

Invitation Ideas

A custom-printed invitation, perhaps very formal and typeset in Old English script, sets the mood best for this party. Or choose formal preprinted fill-in-the-blanks invitations. In either case, include the date, time, location, a reminder to R.S.V.P. with your telephone number, and a detailed explanation of attire. Clarify whether you want guests' dress to represent one of the evening's stories—to come as a character in the story of "The Nutcracker," for example—or in Victorian dress.

Setting the Mood

Decorations: Make the atmosphere warm, gracious, and a bit formal. Light masses of candles in every room and keep Christmas scents wafting through your home (with pots of potpourri simmering on the stove). Dress rooms elegantly but simply: lots of greenery, wreaths, and lovely large bows in gold, silver, red, and green. Decorate a live tree with old-fashioned ornaments such as bows, pine cones, bells, and tiny unlit candles in bright metallic holders.

Music: The only type of music you need is old-fashioned Christmas songs and carols playing softly in the background. Turn off the music during storytelling.

Enhancements: Set the stage in the dining room with place cards, fine china, crystal, and gleaming silver. As a memento of the evening, present guests with a small book of Christmas stories to take home and enjoy!

Special Activities

The evening revolves around listening to tales of Christmases past related by a professional storyteller. For one in your area, check with your local library or a bookstore for information. Or contact one of the following guilds:

The National Storytelling Association
P.O. Box 309
Jonesboro, Tennessee 37659
Telephone 800-525-4514 or 615-753-2171

The National Story League
(formerly the Storyteller's League)
c/o Miss Virginia Dare Shope, President
1342 Fourth Avenue Junieta
Altura, Pennsylvania 16601
Telephone 814-942-3449

In southern California, contact:

South Coast Storytellers Guild
c/o Jim Lewis, Director
P.O. Box 333
Dana Point, California 92629
Telephone 714-496-1960

Should you choose to read or ask a capable guest to do so, some old Christmas favorites to consider are as follows:
• *Amahl and the Night Visitors* by Gian Carlo Menotti
• *Christmas Day in the Morning* by Pearl S. Buck
• *The Gift of the Magi* by O. Henry
• *A Miserable, Merry Christmas* by Lincoln Steffens
• *Mr. Edwards Meets Santa Claus* by Laura Ingalls Wilder
• *The Nutcracker* by Ernst Theodor Amadeus Hoffmann
• *The Other Wise Man* by Henry Van Dyke
• *The Tale of Three Trees—A Traditional Folktale* retold by Angela Elwell Hunt

Theme Variations

Share dinner at an elegant, turn-of-the-century-motif restaurant. After dinner, everyone retires to your home for coffee, after-dinner beverages, and storytelling. This approach works best if your friends are not the type to be intimidated by appearing in public in costume.

Limitations and Logistics

The number of guests is limited only by the size of your home. Eight is a good number for a small house; a larger one might accommodate forty or more.

If you use a firm in which you have confidence, catering is ideal for an elegant sit-down dinner. If finances are a limitation, reduce food expense by foregoing the cost of a full dinner and substituting hors d'oeuvres and beverages or coffee and dessert. Or prepare the food yourself, soliciting help from friends and recruiting servers from among friends' teen or college-age children. A bountiful menu might include: baron of beef or roast goose, twice-baked potatoes, broccoli with lemon and red pepper flakes, frosted berry mold, crusty French rolls with butter, date pudding with butter sauce, and coffee and tea.

If the fee for a professional storyteller does not fit into your budget, you, your spouse, or a guest who enjoys reading aloud—and does so with excellence—can serve as the evening's reader.

Tales of Christmas Party is ideal for couples, singles, ladies only, or even an office party.

Chapter 5

Little Christmas Eve Party

A Norwegian Christmas Celebration

The ethnic celebrations of Christmas are treasured traditions in many families and add even more significance to the holidays. Little Christmas Eve, Lille Jul Aften, in Norway, is one such event. Norwegian Americans gather in the fellowship hall of their church the night before Christmas Eve—the traditional date—to sing, dance around the Christmas tree, play games in which everyone wins, and share with one another what Christmas means to them.

It's an ideal opportunity to celebrate the Norwegian heritage of friends and neighbors, and you don't have to be Norwegian to enjoy it!

Invitation Ideas

Announcements usually are made to a whole church or specific groups within the church. If additional invitations are necessary, a flyer is perfect and inexpensive—especially for a large number of people. Print flyers on red and decorate with red, white, and blue Norwegian flag stickers. In addition to date and time, include your name, the name and address of the church (or rented facility or home where the party will take place). If the celebration takes place in your home, you may want to add your telephone number and request a reply.

Encourage guests to add a Norwegian detail to their outfit. A hat, jacket, apron, or other item from Norway adds authenticity. Even a small Norwegian lapel flag made of paper will remind others of the origin of this gathering.

Setting the Mood

The atmosphere should be one of celebration and Christian love.

Decorations: A live evergreen tree adorned with Norwegian-made ornaments and Christian symbols such as crosses, angels, doves, and fish is the main decoration for this celebration. The rest of the room can be simply decorated with lots of evergreen branches and wreaths, plus dozens of lighted candles—a Norwegian tradition. Norwegian flags can also be displayed around the room.

Music: This is a party where guests make their own music, singing Norwegian and other traditional carols and Christmas songs as they dance around the tree. At other intervals, play traditional Norwegian Christmas music softly in the background.

Enhancements: As guests leave the celebration, give each individual or couple a small memento of the evening, perhaps a simple Norwegian ornament to decorate their own family Christmas tree and remind them of the evening in years to come.

Special Activities

Just before the celebration begins, a large decorated fir tree is carefully placed in the middle of the room. Everyone joins hands, dances around the tree, and sings— "O Christmas Tree" is a favorite. Tell guests about the tradition of the evergreen, that it symbolizes the undying, everlasting life Christians have through Jesus Christ. As guests rest after the energetic dancing and singing, have someone read the Christmas story from Luke 2.

Hot Potato Norwegian style is next. The idea is to give and serve, as a reminder that Christ serves Christians. Beforehand, wrap up a number of boxes inside one another. Gather guests in a large circle—two circles for an enormous crowd. As a (Norwegian) Christmas song is played, participants rapidly pass the box around the circle. When the music stops, the person holding the box opens it to find a slip of paper or small gift. Slips of paper contain a suggestion for service such as, "Wash a friend's car"; "Baby-sit for a family"; or "Cook dinner for a friend." The person holding the box chooses another guest and tells the group how that individual will be served. For example, "I will wash Inge's car." The small gift, similarly, is given to someone else at the celebration. The music and passing of the boxes continues until the final gift is opened.

Theme Variations

At the beginning of the party ask guests to think about a gift they would like to give from the heart: a promise concerning service to others, a check written to a philanthropic organization, and so on. At one point in the evening, ask everyone to share their gift from the heart.

If an ethnic theme other than Norwegian is more appealing to you, share the fun of the traditions of your own heritage with friends.

Limitations and Logistics

Space is the primary restriction on this party. If the church meeting room is expansive, there should be no problem. If you hold the party in your home, however, and it's quite small, the number of guests should be limited accordingly, perhaps twelve to twenty. With simple refreshments, expenses should be rather minimal.

Refreshments at this gathering can be a simple dessert and beverage served buffet style. Norwegians traditionally serve juice or coffee, *Risengrøt* (rice porridge), and *Lefse* (potato crepes). You can use traditional recipes to prepare these or substitute a simple iced cake—in honor of Christ's birthday—with several almonds baked into it. Tradition says that those who get the pieces with almonds win a prize. The prize can be a Norwegian Christmas tree ornament.

Lille Jul Aften was introduced to me by Sam and Kim Casazza, of Long Beach, California. (Kim is of Norwegian heritage.)
Little Christmas Eve Party is a great party for couples, singles, ladies only, and families.

Chapter 6

Chestnuts Roasting on an Open Fire Party

I f you have a fireplace, capitalize on it! Make your hearth the focal point for the whole party. It's the perfect place to gather, relax, and share a friendly meal. Add the fun of good friends reminiscing about Christmases past—the evening's main activity—the mellow tones of Bing Crosby and other forties pop stars, and chestnuts roasting on an open fire. It's a mix that can't miss.

Invitation Ideas

Make your own invitations on casual note paper, or try to find invitations picturing a fireplace. For either, encourage guests to dress in casual clothes, comfortable for sitting on the floor. Add a nostalgic element to the party by asking guests to dress in forties attire—or choose an era when you or the majority of your guests were teens.

If finances are a challenge, cut down on food costs by asking each individual or couple to bring an item to complete your dinner menu. Most guests are delighted to do so! Be specific.

For instance, "Please bring one-half pound of Gruyere cheese, shredded, for our fondue dinner."

Setting the Mood

Decorations: Decorate your home traditionally, with wreaths, garlands, and so on—but highlight these with chestnuts and other nuts. Serve nuts, especially chestnuts, in bowls around the room. Set up your Christmas tree in the party room, and add strings of popcorn and cranberries to your family decorations. The fireplace should receive special decorative attention, since it will be the focal point of the evening—perhaps an all-nut wreath over the mantelpiece. Keep the hearth relatively clear for the activities surrounding the fire.

Music: Emphasize nostalgia! Background music must include Christmas standards such as "White Christmas" and other Bing Crosby favorites. Provide simple song sheets so everyone can sing along if they wish.

Enhancements: If guests want more activity than simple reminiscing and sharing, suggest a game such as Progressive Poetry. (See details at the end of this chapter.)

As an extra precaution at this party, make sure that you have at least two functioning fire extinguishers handy. Accidents can happen.

Special Activities

The evening really revolves around food to an extent. Plan a fondue dinner so that guests can enjoy their meal seated on the floor. (Add a tossed green salad and crusty French bread.) Group everyone around low tables right in front of the fire. Use color-coded skewers, one color per person. Set up everything ahead of time, with dinner and dessert organized. This includes as many fondue pots and utensils as you'll need, as well as all the ingredients (with the exception of those brought by guests). For dessert serve brownies dipped in a peppermint fondue or fresh fruit and cake squares in chocolate fondue. Roasting marshmallows and chestnuts is a must-do activity after the meal. With these details out of the way, you are free to join in the food and fun, and enable others to do so, too!

Encourage each guest to share "Why Christmas has become meaningful to me." You'll find friends love telling about family Christmas traditions and sharing what the holiday really means to them. You might start off by sharing your own thoughts about the meaning of Christmas in order to encourage the relaxed atmosphere.

Theme Variations

To simplify even further, go for virtually no preparation. Purchase only a few items and keep cleanup easy: switch the menu to hot dogs on buns, chips, and a wide assortment of condiments. The whole crowd cooks their own hot dogs and assembles their own all-American s'mores for dessert. (Marshmallows, chocolate squares, and graham crackers—just in case you have never tasted these at camp.)

Limitations and Logistics

The size of the room in your home which has a fireplace is the only limitation; close and cozy is okay but don't be cramped. Up to twenty guests still keep the numbers intimate. Atmosphere is critical: the more you can do to make guests feel comfortable, relaxed, and welcome, the better the party!

Chestnuts Roasting on an Open Fire Party is an especially successful party for couples or singles—or for a small office party.

P.S. Progressive Poetry Party

Give every guest a sheet of paper and a pencil, and instruct them to write an original line of poetry—with a Christmas theme. Then ask everyone to fold the paper over the line, tell the neighbor to the left the last word of the line, and pass on the paper. The neighbor, not knowing the previous line, adds a second line to rhyme with the first. These, again, are folded over and passed to the left for another line, and so on. Each time, the neighbor knows only the last word of the preceding line. When the poems have been full circle, each person reads aloud the complete "Christmas poem" that has returned to him.

Chapter 7

Share the Joy of Christmas Party

racticing the true spirit of Christmas—passing along to others a small part of the blessings and wealth you have received—is the focus of this party. After dinner at an elegant restaurant, guests gather at your home, each bringing a beautiful gift for a silent auction. The proceeds are donated to a charity.

Invitation Ideas

Formal printed invitations seem the right choice for this party. Choose the paper stock and give the printer the exact text. Include the name and address of the restaurant where the guests are to meet as well as your home address (especially for individuals who can only make it to the last half of the party). This is definitely an R.S.V.P. party, so include your telephone number. In addition, specify dress (semiformal or even formal). Or, if you live in an area of the country where people usually dress very casually, specify "coat and tie" so everyone will dress up more than usual.

Ask guests to bring their checkbooks and a generous (unwrapped) gift, perhaps a beautiful piece of art, a coffee table book, or some other special item. This may be a certificate for a sought-after service available within the community, tickets to popular theatrical or sporting events, and so on. Guests' imaginations are the only limits! (Clearly specify whether each individual or each couple is to bring a gift.) Be sure the name of the organization you've earmarked appears on your invitations to be certain everyone understands where the proceeds from the silent auction will be directed.

Setting the Mood

Decorations: If you've already decorated with a beautiful live tree, greenery, wreaths, and perhaps topiaries twinkling with tiny white Christmas lights, the look will be very festive and romantic. Add elegance with tall tapers in candelabra and lovely fresh bouquets of flowers in a scheme of red and white. A bountiful assortment of flowers should enhance the spirit of grace and generosity.

Music: Christmas songs and carols should play softly so as not to distract guests from socializing or bidding.

Enhancements: Brief thank-you notes expressing your appreciation for your guests' generosity to your chosen charity is a nice touch (perhaps during the week following the party). Also let them know you included their name when you made the donation.

Special Activities

Sharing an elegant meal together at a restaurant should set a warm, gracious, and generous tone for the remaining half of the evening. As guests arrive at your home after dinner, quickly arrange all gift items and certificates on display tables, set up ahead of time just for this purpose. Place a small card and a pen next to each gift. Announce clearly a specific closing time for the bidding.

Guests socialize and survey the gifts, writing down on the accompanying cards any generous bid they want to make. They may return to an item again and again, writing in higher and higher bids—silently outbidding one another on the cards—until the host announces, "Bidding is now complete!" (As guests circulate, serve coffee and tea, cappuccino or punch, and offer a tray of assorted Christmas cookies.)

The highest bidder for each item receives his or her gift and writes out a check to the charity of your choice. Checks are collected and tallied immediately so that you can make an announcement before the guests leave: the grand total to be donated to charity. This should bring an added note of satisfaction for guests—that they have participated in a worthwhile cause!

Limitations and Logistics

Your budget is the main restriction for this party. It may be wise to set a limit on what you wish to spend. Ask only the number of guests that can be accommodated within your limit once you've talked with the restaurant about your dinner menu. Further, you might wish to secure a private room, if one is available at the restaurant.

Twelve to forty (even sixty) guests, depending on the size of your home and your budget, can be invited to this party. The more guests you include, the more proceeds will go to your charity. Both a first-class restaurant and a spacious home set an ideal stage for the event, and an atmosphere of loving generosity on the part of the host and hostess, in turn, sets a charitable and unselfish example.

This party is difficult in a small home if you wish to have numerous guests. But even a modest home is adequate. Space can be limited and still be sufficient since guests will be milling about rather than being seated.

Decide ahead of time to which charitable or philanthropic organization you wish to donate the proceeds of the evening. Any deserving group that holds a special place in your heart is perfect.

Share the Joy of Christmas Party is great for couples, singles, an office group, or as a benefit party.

Chapter 8

Christmas Caroling Progressive Party

Do you love giving parties? Do you wish you could find a way to share some of the responsibilities of hosting with others? This Christmas Caroling Progressive Party is your answer. Several neighbors—ideally three to five—host the festivities, with parts of the celebration taking place at each of their homes. (More than three to five makes planning unmanageable and the party schedule unreasonable.) Everyone eats and carols their way through the neighborhood.

Invitation Ideas

Simple flyers on green or red might be illustrated with a small neighborhood map showing houses along the route with host family names, street numbers, and time the crew will arrive at each house. Ask guests to R.S.V.P. by a specific date to the coordinating family, and include your phone number (so you can provide hostesses with an accurate head count). Also, ask guests to bring an inexpensive wrapped gift (under five dollars, for example) suited for either a man or woman. If your climate warrants it, remind everyone to plan for outdoor caroling and to dress accordingly. Your invitation might read:

JOIN US FOR A CHRISTMAS CAROLING PROGRESSIVE PARTY
December 17th
3:00 P.M. at the Thomas home, 4 McCormick,
for snacks and a craft
5:00 P.M. at the Sterling home, 12 McCormick,
for appetizers and Christmas games
7:00 P.M. at the Witt home, 23 McCormick,
for supper and gift exchange
(bring a gift under $5)
and
9:00 P.M. at the Steyer home, 28 McCormick,
for dessert and neighborhood caroling

We're looking forward to seeing you!
Please R.S.V.P. by December 10
to the Thomases for all or as many houses as you can make
Telephone 534-7104

Setting the Mood

Decorations: If each host home is already gaily decorated for the holidays—and there's a roaring fire wherever possible—guests will feel welcome. Red, white, and green helium balloons add to the festive atmosphere, too. A similarly decorated wreath or other festive ornament on each host's front door welcomes guests and lets them know they're at the right houses. Light the pathway at each host home with luminaries (long-lasting candles safely set in sand inside decorative containers)—a wonderful addition.

Music: Have a skilled guitarist, if you know one, accompany the carolers. Your group will fill the evening with their own music. Give the guitarist a break at host homes with a background of recorded Christmas songs and carols.

Special Activities

House Number One: Guests arrive midafternoon for punch and popcorn. Everything needed to complete a simple craft project is supplied by the host and hostess. The project can be simple—an unfinished wood ornament for guests to paint, for example. (Refer to the Resources at the end of this book for suggested crafts books.) At the planned time, simple, duplicated song sheets are handed out, and everyone bundles up and carols their way to the second house.

House Number Two: Guests arrive at approximately 5:00 P.M., ready for simple appetizers and games. Guests can play Christmas Charades—pantomiming well-known Christmas stories, events, and carols—or a game such as Pictionary using only Christmas themes. Hosts and guests then carol their way to the third house.

House Number Three: Guests arrive at approximately 7:00 P.M., ready for a hearty winter supper and gift exchange. The main course should be ready on arrival. Everyone can then go right into exchanging gifts. (A wise hostess will have on hand a few extras, perhaps gag gifts, in case anyone forgets to bring a present.) Everyone draws a gift from Santa's bag. Guests can keep or swap the gifts they draw. Again, hosts and guests carol their way to the next house.

House Number Four: Guests arrive at approximately 9:00 P.M. and build their own hot fudge or brownie sundaes. (Serve hot beverages, too.) Amidst conversation and fun, hosts hand out candles—with paper "skirts" at the base of each candle to protect hands—or flashlights, guests don their outerwear, and everyone makes a final caroling round in the neighborhood. After the final Christmas carol, guests depart for their own homes.

Theme Variations

This celebration can be abbreviated and simplified, eliminating any of the activities, substituting nibbles for a full meal, or spending less time at each home. Do whatever makes this gathering a memorable and joyful celebration for everyone involved!

Women can bring a gift for another woman and men can bring a man's gift. The gifts go into separate Santa sacks, with the men drawing from one and the women drawing from the other.

Limitations and Logistics

Get together with the other hosts—a total of four is a good number—around the first of November to lay out long-range plans. These include planning and dividing up the menu, creating fun activities, putting together a guest list, and setting up a time schedule designed so guests won't stay too long at any one house (and so those who can only make it for part of the celebration will know exactly where and when they can join in).

Send out invitations six to eight weeks in advance. Everyone on the guest list can make this great house-to-house celebration a neighborhood priority, while more distant neighbors can plan their own parties—anticipating the carolers' arrival.

Restrictions are few: Each home must have some type of family room or eating area large enough to accommodate hosts and guests. Weather is another concern. Assuming all of the participants live in the same neighborhood, however, only an Arctic blizzard would be bad enough to cancel this celebration! (A wise hostess will gather up a few extra pairs of mittens, hats, heavy coats, and scarves just in case anyone forgets.)

Finally, since each of the host couples prepares only a portion of the meal, finances should not be a problem for anyone. The menu is planned with a "make-it-in-advance" mindset so that no one is stuck in the kitchen missing the festivities. At every house use festive, disposable paper and plastic ware—to make cleanup easy. A table is necessary only at the home where the main dish is served.

Christmas Caroling Progressive Party is good as a couples, singles, or family party.
Christmas Caroling Progressive Party idea comes from Greg and Elizabeth Thomas, of Irvine, California.

Chapter 9

Sounds of Christmas Party

The main focus of this party is giving—giving to others, who are less fortunate, of our wealth—and even more important—of ourselves, our time.

Have guests gather at your home early in the evening, just after dinner. With song sheets and children's gifts in hand, pile everyone into vans and cars to drive to your city's Ronald McDonald House or a homeless shelter for families. Your evening's activities are simple and fulfilling: interacting with ill children and their families, singing carols, giving the children small gifts, and decorating and sharing Christmas cookies.

Then everyone returns to your home and helps themselves to simple snacks and beverages. Caroling—to accompaniment—may continue if everyone is in the mood. Don't be surprised, however, if poignant discussion follows the earlier highlight of the evening.

An added benefit to this type of party: Guests recognize the needs of the organization, and some may decide to volunteer and help on a regular basis!

Invitation Ideas

Simple flyers duplicated on red or green paper and store-bought invitations are suitable choices. Include your name and address, and also that of the organization and its facility (for stragglers), plus the date and exact time you plan to meet together and leave the house. Suggest comfortable, casual clothes—"Christmas sweaters," if you wish. Ask guests to bring small wrapped gifts for children and/or a snack for the party.

Setting the Mood

Decorations: If your home is already decorated with a pretty Christmas tree, a manger scene, garlands, wreaths, and other ornaments, the festive tone is all set. The focus should definitely be on the spirit of giving, not on trying to impress your guests with a showy house.

Music: Guests' singing provides the music as they carol—perhaps to the accompaniment of a guitar or some other instrument at the organization's facility. (Keys make great jingle bells!) Invite any skilled musicians to bring along their instruments. At your home, ask a skilled pianist to play—if you have a piano. (Guests may wish to stand around the piano and sing on and on!) If no instrumentalists are available, recorded Christmas music will do fine.

Special Activities

Interacting with and singing to the residents of a benevolent organization (i.e., residents of a homeless shelter) are the most important activities of the evening. Hand out simple duplicated song sheets (and perhaps Santa hats!) and briefly convey pertinent rules to guests before loading up to go to your destination.

Because organizations vary in their rules for visitors, go with the flow. If last-minute changes or minor crises occur among residents, remain cheerful and complete whatever activities you are able: singing, touring the building, giving gifts, preparing and eating little snacks, and visiting with the residents. You may want to leave the facility shortly before the rest of the guests to start a roaring fire, heat up beverages, and prepare the house to welcome back your guests.

The Team Caroling Game is very appropriate for this party: Divide into groups of three to eight (if it's a larger party). Each team writes down every Christmas carol of which they can sing two or more lines. Going around in a circle, each team sings one carol they have written down. Other teams must cross off that song from their list. At the end, the team with the greatest number of carols remaining on their list wins! (Award small prizes, such as plates of Christmas goodies, to the winning team.)

Theme Variations

One simple variation on this party: Host it in the afternoon instead of in the evening. If guests are available during the afternoon, this may better meet the schedule of the organization you visit.

Limitations and Logistics

Any number of guests is acceptable, so long as the organization you wish to visit and your home are both large enough to accommodate the crowd. Any local organization, such as a homeless shelter, children's hospital ward or orphanage, or a nursing home is an ideal place to carol. The atmosphere created by the carolers should be one of nonthreatening acceptance and love. (Rise above feeling pity.) Make the arrangements in advance (preferably several weeks or months) for the night of your party—and make notes on timing, optimum number of guests, and restrictions ("No popcorn allowed for certain residents," for example).

Because caroling will be done inside at the benevolent organization's facility, weather will not be a restriction. Should a massive snowstorm block streets in the city, however, reschedule.

Sounds of Christmas Party is a good one for couples, singles, and families as well as an office reach-out project.
Sounds of Christmas Party is the idea of Bill and Cindy Ketner, of Lincoln, Nebraska.

Chapter 10

A Christmas Carol Party

Some people absolutely love costume parties. Charles Dickens's *A Christmas Carol* (1843) makes a great manual for all the details of a holiday costume party. Have guests come dressed as *A Christmas Carol* characters—Ebenezer Scrooge, Bob or Mrs. Cratchitt, Tiny Tim, the Cratchitt daughters Belinda or Martha, or even Jacob Marley's ghost! Arrange for carolers to serenade your guests as you all share a bountiful holiday dinner. After the meal watch a video version of the Dickens story, or have someone who enjoys reading prepare an abbreviated version for your guests' listening pleasure.

As your costume-clad friends leave, say goodnight in the spirit of Tiny Tim: "God Bless Us, Every One!"

Invitation Ideas

Create your own invitations and have them printed. Request Old English script and a formal look, and ask your printer if he has some artwork that would be a reminder of the Dickens story. Preprinted invitations with a formal, old-fashioned flair will also work. In either case include an explanation of the mid-1800s costume to be worn and a reminder to R.S.V.P. with your telephone number. (If guests seem to be at a loss about what costumes might look like, encourage them to explore an encyclopedia, look at illustrations in a library copy of the novel, or talk to a costume rental agency.)

Setting the Mood

Decorations: Your tree and the fireplace mantel (above a roaring fire) can be decorated with old-fashioned memorabilia, Victorian Christmas balls and bows, strings of imitation pearls and beads, and ornaments. Add lots of lighted candles all around the house, and keep the potpourri simmering.

Use a linen tablecloth and napkins, and fine china, crystal, and silver. Vases of fresh Christmas flowers and lots of greenery and tall candles in fancy candelabra will be lovely in the dining room. You can also decorate the table with long strands of imitation pearls and gold or silver beads. A little gold or silver glitter sprinkled over the table adds a final highlight, and, voilà, *A Christmas Carol* setting!

Music: If your community is large enough, contract a group of Dickens-motif carolers several months in advance. Be sure to discuss with them exactly what you want them to sing so that they'll set the desired tone during dinner. If carolers are not available, play old-fashioned Christmas songs in the background during dinner, and lead guests in singing old-fashioned carols at some point during the evening.

Enhancements: The centerpiece can be an ornate sleigh with one small, wrapped gift per guest inside. Attach a streamer to the bow on each package. Carefully direct one streamer (perhaps alternating ribbon colors) to each place setting. When guests finish their meal, each can reel in their streamer to discover a remembrance of the evening.

Special Activities

The serenaded dinner is, of course, a bountiful and festive event. Because it's made even more so by your costumed guests—who have gone to the effort of assembling their Victorian finery—conduct a contest and award prizes for "The Most Authentic Costume," "The Funniest Costume," "The Most Elaborate Costume," and so on.

Theme Variations

Instead of viewing a video of *A Christmas Carol*, lighten up the tone and add a great deal of laughter by substituting your own reenactment of the story. After a brief recount of the plot, have volunteers play the parts of Dickens's major characters. Let them change or modernize the dialogue—or try to talk as they believe Victorians did—producing a hilarious new version of *A Christmas Carol*.

Limitations and Logistics

Two dozen people or more can be invited if you have the space. If space for cooking and serving is limited, keep your guest list to eight to twelve. A large Victorian home is the ideal setting for this party. Since most of us don't live in Victorian mansions, our smaller homes can be transformed into a Victorian-like setting with the right decorations and table settings. Set a warm, inviting welcome tone as you greet each guest at the door with Cratchitt-like hospitality.

The food should be reminiscent of Scrooge's change-of-heart generosity! If finances allow, spring for a caterer. If you prepare the food, kitchen help and servers are a virtual necessity. This meal should be a lovely sit-down dinner with place cards definitely in order. You can serve many more people in much less space, however, if you opt for snacks and beverages rather than a sit-down dinner. The financial investment can also be eased by asking each guest to bring a plate of hors d'oeuvres.

A Christmas Carol *Party is best suited for couples, singles, or office friends.*
A Christmas Carol *Party was originated by Michael and Lisa Brown, of Tustin, California.*

Chapter 11

Love Wrap Party

The focus of this party is on friends gathering together for the joy of giving. They socialize and wrap gifts for others who are in need. The experience brings hope to everyone involved and lasts longer than the gift itself. Hold the party in your home or in a community or church meeting room.

Invitation Ideas

The invitation to this party is more than an invitation. It is actually several printed sheets that explain the details of Love Wrap. The first page explains what Love Wrap is; what happens at the gathering; the date, time, and place it will be held; and what to bring—at least one used item, clean and in good condition, and one canned food item, both unwrapped.

If you make this into a large gathering—the kind that may even require a small committee—host it with like-minded friends. If gifts from those unable to attend can be dropped off prior to the party, list these locations on the invitation, too.

The second page of the invitation lists (approximately) four to ten charities designated to receive the proceeds from the party. Participants can choose in advance the charity to which they want to donate their gifts.

The final page credits donors whose generosity helped make Love Wrap a reality: those who supplied decorations, paper and duplicating for invitations, facilities, wrapping supplies, planning and publicity, entertainment (if applicable), refreshments, drop-off sites, and miscellaneous items and services.

Setting the Mood

Decorations: Simple is best for this celebration of giving. Christmas garlands and wreaths or colorful helium balloons are adequate. Decorate the buffet table simply in traditional Christmas colors—with a lovely Christmas flower arrangement, if one is donated, at the center.

Music: Vocal and instrumental music may be provided by entertainers—or pipe in background Christmas carols and songs.

Enhancements: If many guests have small children and require child care in order to participate, provide a separate playroom with trusted baby-sitters and planned activities for the children.

Special Activities

The main activity of the afternoon is wrapping gifts. Each guest wraps the gift he or she has brought plus gifts that have been donated by those unable to attend. Guests place their gifts and canned goods in areas designated for their chosen charity.

Make light refreshments available throughout the party. If you can do so, arrange for a high school musical group, a small background band, an individual musician or other entertainer. Whoever performs needs to be able to do so without the full attention of guests, so that they can stay busy wrapping gifts.

Theme Variations

☞ Have bags specially printed with the Love Wrap name, location, date, and time, and mail these in an oversized envelope along with the invitation.

☞ Add a small display of photographs of people benefited by each charity. Set them up where gifts are to be placed for that organization.

☞ If your Love Wrap party is small, concentrate on several specific families in need instead of a large charity. Get names and details from agencies ahead of time. Request that guests bring food products, clothes, and toys for specific children in the family. Wrap the gifts and decorate a mini Christmas tree. At the end of your party, deliver the food and presents to the families.

☞ Instead of having your Love Wrap party during the holiday season, you may want to plan your party during February, the love month. By then, with gift giving over, the less fortunate are often forgotten. Bill your celebration as "Christmas in February!"

Limitations and Logistics

The rule—room permitting—for your number of guests is "the more the merrier." A large meeting room such as a church fellowship hall or business conference hall is ideal. Avoid renting a facility. Churches and businesses are often willing to donate space (as well as supplies) for a worthy endeavor. If you choose to have Love Wrap in your home, plan the party in the largest living area, even if it's the basement.

Preparation is crucial. Ask several friends to cohost and plan with you. Depending on the size of the gathering, you may need to plan for months ahead of time securing donations for all aspects of the party: facility, invitations, wrapping supplies, refreshments, decorations, publicity, and (optional) entertainment. Also contact and make arrangements with the charities that will be recipients of the gifts.

Before the party begins, a group will be needed to set up long tables, chairs, and wrapping supplies. Refreshments can also be set up at that time. Make large signs to designate specific areas to place gifts for individual charities.

Simplicity is the key to refreshments: Christmas cookies—donated by bakeries and grocery stores—and punch or coffee.

Love Wrap Party is an ideal reach-out project for any group of people, from singles to office groups to families.
Cruise and Dorraine Palmer of Prairie Village, Kansas, introduced me to Love Wrap Party.

Chapter 12

He Is the Reason for the Season Party

The theme of this gathering is the Nativity. The evening gives adults an opportunity to enjoy fellowship, conversation, and activities that emphasize the true significance of the Christmas story.

As people arrive, tape a sign on the back of each guest naming a person or thing related to the first Christmas. This sets the stage for a terrific icebreaker that allows old and new members of the group to get to know one another better, and is part of a game for the evening as well. As the evening comes to a close, play David Meece's song, "We Are the Reason," a powerful reminder that "Christ is the reason for the season."

Invitation Ideas

A simple flyer or printed invitation works well for this party. However, if time permits, cut invitations in the shape of a gift box out of white card stock. On the gift tag write in red or green, "He Is the Reason for the Season," or "To Jesus with Love." On the reverse side, write in party details. If you want

guests to bring a snack or dessert, add the request, along with a telephone number and R.S.V.P. request. Ask guests to come in casual or dressy attire, depending upon your preference. (If guests are looking for an opportunity to be more formal, encourage everyone to dress up!)

Setting the Mood

Decorations: The one decoration that is a must for this party is a manger. Construct a simple wooden one and fill it with straw from a feed store and set it up at a prominent place in the party room. If you have a Nativity scene, set it up in the room, too, as a reminder of the evening's focus. Decorate your Christmas tree exclusively with Christian symbols: angels, doves, crosses, and fish. On the front door, hang a decorated wreath proclaiming, "He Is the Reason for the Season."

Music: Guests may want to sing a few carols during the evening. In advance, locate a skilled pianist or guitarist in the group to accompany the singing. Hand out duplicated song sheets with the words to Christ-centered Christmas carols. Also secure a copy of David Meece's "We Are the Reason" and other recorded Christmas songs and play them throughout the evening.

Enhancements: My friend Joan Massey adds her unique and special touch. She places an enormous eight-foot wreath on the wall behind her couch. At its center are the words "Jesus Is the Reason for the Season" cut out of Christmas wrap. As the evening progresses, every couple has their picture taken, sitting on the couch with the wreath above their heads. Joan has double prints developed and sends the second copy to the couple the following week, as a loving reminder of the message and the wonderful evening shared together.

Special Activities

The main activities of the evening are times of special sharing about memories and gifts from everyone's past and a creative and fun icebreaker based on the story of the Nativity, from Luke 2. Open the party with a clever paraphrase of the Christmas story. (See the end of this chapter for complete details on how to carry it out.) Because it enables virtually all of the guests to meet one another, it sets a friendly and inclusive tone. After guests enjoy a time of eating and socializing, each person—going around in a large circle—tells the rest of the group one memory or gift that made a Christmas in the past most meaningful. The group may also sing or pray together, if desired.

The menu for this party need not be elaborate. Ask each couple to bring a plate of hors d'oeuvres or snacks. You will prepare a delicious Christmas dessert and offer beverages.

Limitations and Logistics

The only real limitation is the size of the home where the party is held. If the size of the group involved puts a strain on your home, move to a room in your church where you can still build a warm, loving atmosphere.

The "Christmas Story and You" Game

Give everyone a blank copy of the story. Then, give these directions to guests:

1. Pinned to your back is a sign naming a person, place, or thing somehow related to the Christmas story. Your goal is to discover who or what you are by asking questions to which others can answer only "yes" or "no." You may ask only one question per person. When you have discovered who or what you are, fill in the appropriate blank in the story.

2. Then, see how many other blanks you can fill in with the correct names. For example: "Long ago in the city of Nazareth (Will) lived a young girl named Mary (Lindy)." Associate names with faces.

3. The game winner is the first person who has all the blanks filled in correctly and is able to read the story aloud, pointing out each person by name.

Long ago in the city of Nazareth (_____) lived a young girl named Mary (_____).

One day, the angel Gabriel (_____), appeared to Mary and told her she would have a baby who

would be Jesus, the Son of God. Mary was engaged to a young carpenter named Joseph (_____).

Augustus (_____) decreed that all the world should be taxed. Joseph took his wife, Mary, to

Bethlehem (_____). Mary rode on a donkey (_____) led by Joseph. When they

arrived in Bethlehem, all the inns (_____, _____, and _____) were full. One

innkeeper (_____) allowed them to spend the night in his stable (_____). The stable was

full of hay (_____) and animals (cow _____, rooster _____, and chicken

_____). It was there that Mary "brought forth her firstborn son." She wrapped Him in swaddling

clothes (_____) and laid Him in a manger (_____).

In the same country, there were shepherds (_____, _____, and _____) in the fields keeping watch over their flocks (_____, _____, _____, _____, and (_____) by night.

An angel of the Lord (_____) came upon them. Glory shone all around them. "Fear not, for I bring you good tidings of great joy. For unto you is born a Savior, Christ the Lord." Suddenly there appeared a multitude of the Heavenly hosts (_____, _____, _____, _____, _____, and _____).

They said, "Glory to God in the highest... and on earth, peace, goodwill toward men." The shepherds came with haste to worship the baby. They spread the news with great rejoicing, "Christ the Savior is born!"

Three wise men from the east (_____, _____, and _____) came to see Baby Jesus. They rode on camels (_____, _____, and _____) and followed a bright star (_____) which came to rest over the place where Jesus lay. They worshiped the newborn baby and gave Him gifts of gold (_____), frankincense (_____), and myrrh (_____).

He Is the Reason for the Season Party is good for couples and singles, especially from an adult Sunday School class.
Will and Lindy Wilson, of Auburn, California, first told me about the He Is the Reason for the Season party.

Chapter 13

It's a Wonderful Life! Party

I f you want to bring friends together in a relaxing and happy atmosphere to enjoy one another and reflect on the positive aspects of their lives, what better way than to use the beloved film classic *It's a Wonderful Life!* as your party theme?

No one who knows the story can resist the opportunity to view it for even the hundredth time. It's a wonderful way for everyone to step back from the frantic pace and commercialism of Christmas and reflect on the fact that it really is a wonderful life!

Invitation Ideas

Simple duplicated flyers on green or red paper are excellent for this casual gathering. Just fold, staple, and mail. Be sure to use the phrase, "It's a Wonderful Life!" and encourage casual, comfortable dress. Since the gathering is informal, just ask for "regrets only" for a relatively accurate head count. To help guests feel more a part of the festivities, ask them to bring something—a plate of Christmas snacks or a dessert to share.

Setting the Mood

Decorations: Because the television is a focal point for the evening, place some decorated greenery on top. A nicely decorated tree and a roaring fire add lovely touches, too.

Music: Not a major factor in this party, music—perhaps Christmas songs from the 1940s—can be played in the background before and after the film.

Enhancements: Again, with television playing a huge part in your party, a big screen is ideal. These can be rented for an evening for a nominal fee.

Throughout the party, take Polaroid photos of fun times shared by guests. Put them together in a simple picture collage (framed or unframed) for everyone to enjoy, and save them for next year when you throw the party again! (The memories conjured up by the photographs can provide hours of conversation.)

Although the party has plenty of activity, you may also want to have a gift exchange. (See the end of this chapter for a game that distributes the presents in a unique way.)

Special Activities

Food, conversation, and watching *It's A Wonderful Life!* are all you need. But it might interest guests if you read aloud Leonard Maltin's note from his *Movie and Video Reviews:*

> *"It's A Wonderful Life!* (1946), directed by Frank Capra, stars James Stewart and Donna Reed. It is a sentimental tale of Stewart, who works all his life to make good in a small town, but thinks he's failed and tries to end his life. Guardian angel (Henry Travers) comes to show him his mistake. This film seems to improve with age."

After seeing the video, guests may share how the movie relates to their lives. This should be strictly voluntary, with no one under pressure to participate.

Limitations and Logistics

Up to twenty people is an ideal number for this party. If your house or apartment is very small, simply keep the number of invited guests to eight or so.

Although there is not a great deal of preparation needed for the party, take care of securing the video of *It's a Wonderful Life!* (preferably the computer-colored version) for the evening. This should be a relatively simple task due to the enormous popularity and availability of the video. But at Christmas time it might be especially popular at video rental outlets, so reserve ahead. An alternative is to plan the party on an evening when this movie is to be televised.

With guests bringing items, planning is even easier. You might also offer soft drinks and a variety of popcorn flavors—plain, cheese, caramel, cinnamon, and so on—perfect for movie watching! Or add crackers and cheese, hot chocolate, coffee, and tea to your guests' offerings.

Gifts for Doubles Game

1. All guests gather in a circle, at a table or on the floor, with wrapped gifts in the middle.
2. Give a paper plate with two dice on it to every fourth or fifth individual in the circle.
3. Signal for the game to start, and set a timer for ten minutes.
4. Guests each roll the dice on the paper plate, and then pass that plate clockwise.
5. When someone rolls doubles on the dice, he or she chooses a gift from the middle of the table or "steals" a gift from another player.

6. Everyone continues to roll, pass the dice, and choose or steal gifts until the timer rings or all the gifts are taken.
7. Those guests who end up with (one or more) gifts keep them!

It's a Wonderful Life! *Party is a great party for couples, singles and families.*

Chapter 14

Latino Christmas Celebration

The main focus of this celebration is fun. Let your guests know from the minute they receive word of this gathering that it is going to be an uproarious time of socializing, dancing, and celebrating Latino culture and customs.

Try to secure a Latin disc jockey for the evening, and tell guests, "Wear your dancin' shoes!" Ask guests to bring a gag gift for a "white elephant" gift exchange and a plate of Latin-style hors d'oeuvres, such as nachos. Around midnight, serve cake and sweet dark coffee, Latin-style.

Invitation Ideas

Mail out simple green, white, and red invitations (the colors of the Mexican flag) with all the details. For such a large and informal party, no R.S.V.P. is needed. Ask guests to bring a plate of snacks, emphasizing the Latin menu (Mexican, Cuban, Puerto Rican, South and Central American). Also tell everyone to wrap and bring a gag gift for the exchange. Suggest casual, comfortable clothing or attire with a Latin touch, and remind everyone to wear their dancing shoes.

Setting the Mood

Decorations: Start with multitudes of balloon clusters as well as green, white, and red helium balloons—some with numbers inside to be popped for the gift exchange (see Special Activities). Decorate the Christmas tree in bright colors with tin ornaments, tiny dolls made in Mexico, and so on. Hang colorful piñatas and flags from Latin American countries around the room. Remember, you need to leave the majority of the space for dancing.

Music: Have the disc jockey focus on Latin music for dancing the salsa, cumbia, rumba, and so on. You may want a variety of other types of music, too, but intersperse Latin music throughout the evening to retain the Latin flavor.

Special Activities

Dancing, socializing, yummy Latin snacks, and a gag gift exchange are the evening's entertainment. Be sure your disc jockey is excellent and knows the music; he will set the tone for the evening.

As guests arrive—to the sounds of lively Latin strains—take their wrapped gag gifts, attach a stick-on number to each, and put them under the Christmas tree. They can get right on the dance floor when they arrive. After an hour or so, announce that the gag gift exchange is about to begin. Everyone gathers around the Christmas tree, and each guest is handed a green, white, or red balloon with a number inside. Pass around a hat pin, and one at a time, guests pop their balloons and go to the tree to find the matching number on a gift. Each guest opens the present or leaves it wrapped, "steals" someone else's gift, and gives his unopened gift to the person from whom he stole the gift. After the final present is opened, guests can move to the refreshment tables or return to dancing.

Theme Variations

You can make this international Christmas celebration Italian. Substitute Italian music and dancing, foods such as lasagna, and decorations from Italy. (The colors of the Italian flag are the same as those of the Mexican flag.)

Limitations and Logistics

The main restrictions are space and finances. If you want to have a real fiesta with a big crowd, renting a facility and hiring a professional disc jockey for the evening may get quite expensive. If several hosts and hostesses get together and throw this party, however, you can divide the costs and multiply the fun!

Any number of guests is fine, but especially for this gathering, "the more the merrier!" holds true. Because there will probably be a big crowd and lots of Latin dancing, the best location for this celebration is a public space. The atmosphere should be one of merriment and absolute celebration!

If guests ask what to bring, suggest Latin favorites such as ham or chicken croquettes, pastelitos or empanadas, tacos or taquitos, and corn chips and guacamole.

You can provide punch or soft drinks as well as fresh banana or coconut cake and sweet dark coffee for midnight.

If you don't want to ask guests to bring food, or if this is to be an office party, have the food done by a Latin caterer. Either way, serve on colorful paper goods and use plastic ware for easy cleanup.

Latino Christmas Celebration is ideal for couples, singles, and as an office party.
Nacho and Sara Pecina, of Miami, Florida, suggested this Latino Christmas Celebration.

Chapter 15

Christmas Midnight Buffet

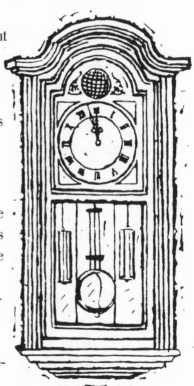

Some people just enjoy being night owls, so a midnight buffet is right up their alley. If you fit into this category, hire a small instrumental group, decorate your home to set the scene for an elegant evening, and send out the invitations for a scrumptious midnight buffet. If you can't seem to get away from the kids and go to formal parties very often, make it black tie and stay up late!

Invitation Ideas

Make the invitation to this party formal and have the invitations done by a commercial printer. Invite guests to a midnight buffet unless you've decided on an additional theme such as "An Evening in the Land of Oz" or "An Evening in the Deep South."

Include your name, address, the date, and both beginning and ending times—perhaps 9:00 P.M. until 1:00 A.M.—as the party starts and concludes late. Instruct guests on appropriate attire for the evening— black tie or a costume theme. Finally, add an R.S.V.P. and your telephone number, with the date by which you would like their response.

Setting the Mood

Decorations: Candlelight and fresh-flower arrangements or groupings of poinsettias should be abundant. Decorate the Christmas tree—or perhaps several smaller trees— in concert with the theme of the party if there is one. Make the mantel beautiful with lots of greenery and ornaments that enhance your theme. Carry out the decorating scheme throughout the house, including numerous candles and Christmas towels in the guest bathroom. Decorate the front of your home invitingly, with luminaria, white lights, poinsettias, and a beautiful wreath or other door decoration to welcome guests.

Music: The small instrumental group you hire to play for the evening should be one that you have heard (if only on cassette) and that comes on the highest recommendation of a trusted friend. The group need not be large; a trio will suffice. A versatile group is best so that guests can enjoy a variety of styles of music. Depending on your taste and that of your guests, however, you might choose a group that specializes in rock or jazz, for example.

Enhancements: Here are several different ideas to add to your celebration:

- ☞ Present a Christmas corsage, traditional or wrist-style, to each woman as she arrives.
- ☞ Arrange to have a professional photographer at the party. Later, send guests a picture of themselves in formal attire in your beautiful setting. (If you or your spouse is particularly good at photography, take these pictures.)
- ☞ Print small menus for the evening and roll them up like miniature scrolls. These make a nice remembrance of the celebration.
- ☞ Hire older children or young adults to take care of valet parking for your guests. Check to see if a permit is needed for parking cars in your neighborhood.
- ☞ Have guests draw a number from a bowl and match it with a number already on a present under the Christmas tree. Each guest receives a special surprise gift!

☛ One host I know of gives wonderful prizes to those who guess the answers to the clue-filled questions he has given out during the evening. This creative host also hands out special door prizes and secures a unique entertainer for the enjoyment of his guests each year—a comedian or magician, even a belly dancer!

Special Activities

Greet guests with a cup of festive punch. Approximately an hour after arrival time, announce that dancing will begin. With plenty of room for dancing and clusters of tables and chairs to invite conversation, guests can alternate between dancing and socializing until almost midnight.

At that time, invite guests to join you for the gala midnight dinner buffet. Guests can take their food and beverages back to the tables and socialize in large or small groups. After they eat, guests can continue to dance until the party is over.

Limitations and Logistics

Eight to twelve couples is an ideal number for this party if it is held in a home, which is the best location to ensure just the right atmosphere. If the gathering is to be an office party, with a large guest list, a charming room at a country club or other banquet facility will afford more space and still work nicely.

Advance preparations are a must for this party. Because entertainers' schedules fill up quickly for the holiday season, book your instrumental group four to six months in advance. Do the same careful scheduling for your caterer so that you can get your first choice on the calendar—and also plan out your menu early. Have all details ironed out and invitation wording at your printer so that invitations are completed and ready to mail at least four weeks in advance.

Both the size of your home and the size of your budget may present challenges. Presumably, if this is an office party, neither will be insurmountable. If individuals are planning this party, however, I suggest you join with several couples to cohost the party and split the costs. If several host couples are involved, have a brief meeting in late summer or early fall to assign various tasks. This kind of organization will pay great dividends as the party date comes closer. Limit your guest list to whatever number you feel will be comfortable in the home or facility you choose.

This party is meant to be catered. With a large number of guests, this is almost a must. It allows the hostess(es) to enjoy the evening and the guests, and eliminates setup and cleanup, too. If catering is not feasible, plan the menu around food that can be prepared almost exclusively ahead of time. Working together, the host couples can share food costs, as well as menu and cooking responsibilities, and plan a beautiful buffet table, perhaps using holiday linens and Christmas china. A fresh Christmas flower arrangement can serve as an attractive centerpiece. (Note: If you are using an additional theme, plan your menu around it.)

If the party is not catered, trade off serving at the holiday parties of friends. I know a woman who joined with five others to do this. Each made a simple black satin skirt and all bought identical white blouses. As each hosted her own Christmas party, the other five served in the kitchen and at the buffet table. Thus, everyone had all the help they needed!

Christmas Midnight Buffet is suitable for couples, singles, and office groups.
Stefan and Holly Demetrescu, of Irvine, California, hold a Christmas Midnight Buffet like this.

Chapter 16

Not Another Christmas Banquet! Party

ave you ever thought to yourself, I would pay to not go to another Christmas party? Well, the idea of this noncelebration is to raise money in a clever and unique way.

In lieu of spending money on one more party they may not want to attend anyway, your friends and acquaintances become nonguests and support the excellent work of your favorite charity. I assure you, they will be delighted to stay away from this unique party.

Invitation Ideas

Set a fictitious date for your nonparty, perhaps December 24 or December 25, and proceed to plan details that won't need to be carried out—except in your imagination. Have a printer make up formal invitations, response cards, and preaddressed stamped envelopes (to the charity you have chosen). This is the only cost of your nonevent!

Include the name of your nonprofit organization or charity. Also include the names of the organization leaders, so recipients will recognize the connection and validity of the request.

There is no need to tell guests how to dress, since they won't be attending. Obviously, no R.S.V.P. is necessary either, but be sure to include your fabricated date, time, and made-up address (the North Pole?) for your nonexistent party.

Also be sure to include a simple but thorough explanation of the purpose of the fundraiser and why you are sending out these invitations and response cards instead of asking them to one more Christmas party. (Note: If you wish, set a suggested donation, such as ten dollars or one hundred dollars a plate for your nonexistent sit-down dinner.)

Before using their names, commit your speaker, singers, and musicians to not show up so that you can safely use their names in your invitation—and in the publicity for this project. Remember to send out invitations not only to guests, but also to the speaker, musicians, and singers who have committed themselves not to perform at one more gathering!

Setting the Mood

Decorations: None
Music: None
Enhancements: None

Special Activities

None

Theme Variations

Make personal phone calls to people and ask them to "say no to attending one more Christmas party." In lieu of attending another gathering in the already-too-hectic holiday season, guests are invited to simply send a check to support your favorite charity, while they stay home and enjoy an evening with their families.

Limitations and Logistics

None

Not Another Christmas Banquet! Party is a good benefit for any group of friends or associates. Tim Thomas, Baptist Student Union Director for the Mississippi Gulf Coast Community Colleges came up with Not Another Christmas Banquet! Party.

Chapter 17

Chinese Christmas Party

Many people want a unique idea for their Christmas party. Chinese Christmas Party is certainly that! Treat guests to a delicious dinner at a well-known Chinese restaurant, then everyone goes to your home. A warm, inviting atmosphere—like the graciousness and hospitality of the Chinese—greets guests as they place their handmade gifts under the tree. When everyone has arrived, it's time for the Chinese gift exchange to begin. Afterward, as guests admire one another's handmade presents, bring out Chinese tea and fortune cookies.

Invitation Ideas

Invitations can be custom-made, printed in red ink, and decorated with Chinese symbols and artwork on them. If you can find a preprinted one with an Oriental look, it will do very well. In addition to your name, be sure to include the name and address of the Chinese restaurant where guests are to meet, your home address, the date and time of the party, and how to dress. Insert a date by which you need an R.S.V.P. from everyone along with your telephone number. Ask each guest to bring a wrapped gift—made by hand.

Of course, guests can simply wear attire that is appropriate to your choice of Chinese restaurant. Why not carry out the Chinese theme a bit further, however? Ask guests to wear a costume that represents the Chinese Lunar Sign year of their birth. (See Chinese Lunar Signs from 1900 to 2007 at the end of this chapter.) Or ask them to bring costumes to don for the after-dinner festivities in your home. Award prizes for the "Most Authentic Costume," the "Funniest Costume," and so on.

Setting the Mood

Decorations: Carry out the Chinese theme in every way possible in your decorations. Make red your predominant color. It's indicative of joy and good fortune to the Chinese. Decorate your whole Christmas tree in red, or add ornaments such as small Chinese umbrellas. Greenery intertwined with red lights and Chinese lanterns wherever possible can decorate other locations in the house. Welcome guests at the front door with a wreath or sign with the words *"Sheng Dan Kuai Le,"* which is "Merry Christmas" in Chinese.

Music: If possible, obtain cassettes or compact discs of Chinese music. Even though Christmas is not observed in China as we know it in the United States, the Chinese love music. And Chinese holiday sounds, played softly in the background, add authenticity and joy to the mood of the evening.

Special Activities

When guests arrive at your home and place their wrapped handmade gifts or crafts under the Christmas tree, have them draw a number out of a bowl. This sets the stage for the Chinese gift exchange. It takes place in the same manner as a "white elephant" gift exchange. The one difference is that since every present has been made by hand, many will be unique and beautiful—so there may be a great deal of "stealing" of one another's gifts that takes place. (See the White Elephant Party chapter for details.)

As a finale to the evening—and a simple dessert—guests can enjoy fortune cookies and read aloud their "fortunes" to the group. It's sure to bring laughter as the evening closes.

Theme Variations

Serve a catered Chinese meal in your home instead of hosting your guests in a restaurant. One suggestion for implementing this is to have the caterers set up several different "stations" in or near the dining area. Everyone selects their own ingredients, and the chefs create custom stir-fry for each guest!

Limitations and Logistics

In preparation for the party, once you've received a response from each of the invitees, make a reservation at an excellent Chinese restaurant, preferably in a separate reserved room for this purpose. Do this as early as possible, to be sure you get your first choice of date and time. Guests meet at the restaurant at the given time. As everyone finishes dinner, the host should announce that the party will depart for home.

The primary restriction on this party will be finances. Treating a large number of guests to dinner at a high-quality Chinese restaurant may be costly, if not prohibitive. To solve this problem, several hosts and hostesses can go together and split the restaurant bill. Or, you might compare the cost of having the party catered in your home to the cost of dinner for all your guests at the restaurant. A final possibility? Ask a friend who is skilled at Chinese cooking to give a quick course so you (and any other hostesses) can try your hand at preparing the food. Then, the only concern is the size of your house. Simply restrict your guest list to a number that will comfortably fit into your home.

Assuming that the food will be served at a restaurant or catered, your only preparation is to have available an assortment of Chinese teas and some commercially made fortune cookies. Both are available from an import store, and may be found in the specialty section of a supermarket, depending upon your community. (Heat up plenty of water at the appropriate time, before it's time to serve the tea.)

Chinese Lunar Signs from 1900 to 2007

Find the year you were born on this chart and dress in a costume representing the animal listed:

RAT	1900	1912	1924	1936	1948	1960	1972	1984	1996
OX	1901	1913	1925	1937	1949	1961	1973	1985	1997
TIGER	1902	1914	1926	1938	1950	1962	1974	1986	1998
RABBIT	1903	1915	1927	1939	1951	1963	1975	1987	1999
DRAGON	1904	1916	1928	1940	1952	1964	1976	1988	2000
SNAKE	1905	1917	1929	1941	1953	1965	1977	1989	2001
HORSE	1906	1918	1930	1942	1954	1966	1978	1990	2002
SHEEP	1907	1919	1931	1943	1955	1967	1979	1991	2003
MONKEY	1908	1920	1932	1944	1956	1968	1980	1992	2004
ROOSTER	1909	1921	1933	1945	1957	1969	1981	1993	2005
DOG	1910	1922	1934	1946	1958	1970	1982	1994	2006
BOAR	1911	1923	1935	1947	1959	1971	1983	1995	2007

A Chinese Christmas Party is fun for couples, singles, and as an office gathering.
John and Melony Puz of Beaumont, Texas, came up with this party.

Chapter 18

It's Time to Decorate Your House Party

Supply all the fixings for guests to create their very own start-to-finish, custom-built gingerbread houses, and you've got a winning Christmas party. Simply set up tables and chairs, purchased gingerbread house kits, icing, and enough varied candy to sink a battleship. Before you know it, everyone will be competing to make theirs the most spectacular gingerbread house of all!

And lest everyone is tempted to devour their masterpieces, serve a variety of snacks and beverages. At the evening's close, send guests home with their gingerbread houses. They'll all go away from the evening feeling like a master builder!

Invitation Ideas

Creative store-bought invitations, perhaps with a Santa's Village or gingerbread motif on them, are perfect. Or, cut out small gingerbread houses from brown kraft paper, and use colored markers to decorate them. In addition to the usual information, request an R.S.V.P. and give your telephone number so that you'll have enough supplies on hand.

Ideal dress for this party is casual. There is no reason to dress up and every reason to suggest clothes that will withstand the rigors of frosting. If anyone arrives dressed up, the wise hostess has some aprons on hand to protect guests' clothes.

Setting the Mood

Decorations: The gingerbread houses will be wonderfully colorful and fun decorations. Little else needs to be added if traditional Christmas decorations are already in place—a brightly decorated tree, wreaths, greenery, a cheery fire in the fireplace. One clever note: Small gingerbread men and lots of colorful candies can be hung or strung on the tree or wired into your decorative greenery and wreaths—to carry out the theme.

Music: Recorded Christmas songs played in the background are enough. But encourage guests, if they wish, to break out and sing along with the Christmas carols while they decorate their gingerbread houses.

Enhancements: Guests take home their masterpieces—for their children or others to enjoy or even nibble on!

Special Activities

The main focus of this party is the creation of original gingerbread houses. Before guests start, provide a few simple instructions, such as, "Follow the directions on the kits for assembling the houses. Work on one wall at a time so that the frosting mortar won't harden too quickly," and so on. Give hints now and then as everyone proceeds: "Make a perfect snowman using three large marshmallows," or "Shredded coconut on top of the roof icing makes wonderful snow." Encourage new levels of creativity! (There's no need to warn guests against candy tasting—they will soon discover how quickly they tire of the sweet taste.)

After everyone is finished, award prizes for the house that is "Tackiest," "Most Symmetrical," "Most Majestic," "Funniest," "Most Tempting to Eat," and so on. (Be creative with your awards.) Plates of decorated gingerbread men are excellent prizes. After the awards, direct guests to snacks and beverages.

Theme Variations

If the cost of purchasing gingerbread house kits for a large number of guests is prohibitive, bake your own—if you have the intestinal fortitude—or use alternative materials for the basics: graham crackers adhered to a milk carton with a hot glue gun, or even a sturdy shoe box with its lid folded to make a roof. Covered with "frosting mortar," no one will know the difference!

Limitations and Logistics

The number of guests is limited only by the table space or other work areas in your home. Twelve to twenty is, perhaps, ideal. A home is the obvious place to host such a gathering, due to the need for kitchen facilities, tabletop areas, and so on.

In order for this party to go smoothly, careful ahead-of-time preparation is wise. Mail order or purchase a gingerbread house kit for every two to four people. (Swiss Colony will mail high-quality gingerbread house kits to you; check with a local Swiss Colony or similar store or catalog. Less elaborate kits can also be purchased at Christmastime at stores such as Target.) Check beforehand to be sure kits will have adequate "frosting mortar." It's probably wise to whip up several extra recipes of it (see appendix for recipe). If graham cracker-and-milk-carton or shoe-box versions are to be constructed, be sure to have these supplies on hand instead.

Many gingerbread house kits are quite skimpy on extra candies, so purchase a large variety of edible decorations, including candies. Fill a small bowl of each variety at every table. Here are some suggestions:

- Mixed nuts in shells
- Peppermint candies
- Red hots
- Small jelly beans
- Red and/or black licorice
- Candy wafers

- Candy canes and/or sticks
- Mini and large marshmallows
- Candy mints
- Teddy bear cookies
- Silver candy balls
- Multicolored sprinkles

- Gumdrops
- M & Ms
- Gummy Bears
- Life Savers
- Hershey Kisses
- Mini Oreo cookies

Be sure there is plenty of tabletop space and a chair available for each guest. (Even good wood tables, covered with plastic tablecloths, can be used.) Cover a sturdy square of cardboard or foam core with aluminum foil—for carrying and easy cleanup purposes. Finally, it is best to work in rooms that have easy-clean floors.

Set up your buffet table with snacks and beverages that are not sweet; guests will soon understand why. Vegetables and dip, crackers and cheeses, chips, and other similar munchies will provide a welcome change of taste. You can also decorate the serving table with—then eat—gingerbread men. Offer frosty mugs of milk and mugs or cups of coffee, tea, and hot chocolate.

It's Time to Decorate Your House Party is perfect for couples, singles, office friends, and families!
It's Time to Decorate Your House Party was introduced to me by Allen and Susan Lavelle, of Irvine, California.

Chapter 19

Hats off to Christmas! Party

For a terrific party with an emphasis on the creative, put together a mountain of craft supplies, from construction paper to pipe cleaners, and have guests make the wildest, craziest hats they can—with a holiday flair. After a hat-judging contest with funny prizes, serve snacks and hand out paper and pens or pencils for Letters to Santa. Be sure to have on hand a distinctive hat to pass around to collect funds for a worthwhile charity, too. Then, your favorite organization will benefit from the fun just as your guests have.

Invitation Ideas

If time permits, make your own invitations: Cut top hat shapes from green or red construction paper or card stock and print "Hats Off to Christmas!" on the front. An R.S.V.P. with your phone number is probably best for this party (so you're sure to have enough craft supplies on hand). Request that guests bring a plate of Christmas snacks or hors d'oeuvres to share with the group. Add a brief note to inform them that they'll have the opportunity at your party to contribute to the charity you have chosen (so that they'll be prepared to give if they so choose).

Setting the Mood

Decorations: Hats are the decoration of the evening. Place Christmas hats, as well as hats of all varieties from all over the world on your walls and all around your party room. For a centerpiece, put flowers in a small waterproof container and place flowers and "vase" inside an upside-down hat. Decorate greenery, wreaths, the mantel, your Christmas tree, and so on throughout your house with tiny imitation hats. Enhance a man's or woman's hat with small Christmas decorations and hang it on the front door to welcome your guests!

Music: At some point in the evening, guests may want to break into a spontaneous round of Christmas carols. Great! If not, the only music you need is that of recorded Christmas songs and carols in the background.

Special Activities

As soon as guests arrive, direct them to the craft supplies you've laid out. Encourage them to construct a Santa hat, creative earmuffs, reindeer antlers, or whatever. The only limit is their ingenuity. Whenever they wish, guests can help themselves to light snacks and beverages. After guests have completed and modeled their hats, ask the group, by their applause, to award category prizes— "Wildest Hat," "Most Creative Use of Materials," "Ugliest Hat," and so on. Then pass the hat. Both winners and losers contribute to your charity.

Afterward, announce that Letters to Santa is about to begin. With a list of the names of your guests in hand, have each guest individually whisper to you which other guest on whose behalf he or she would like to write a fictitious "Dear Santa" letter, and write one's name next to the other (to be sure each guest gets only one letter). Give each guest a sheet of paper, a pen or pencil, and approximately five minutes to write a brief, humorous (positive) letter on behalf of the person they've chosen. A boyfriend, for example, might write—supposedly from his girlfriend—"Dear Santa, I sure wish my boyfriend would pop the question!" Or a girl might write—supposedly from her roommate—"Dear Santa, Could you please send a handsome guy over to my house to fix my toilet?" After time is up, ask guests to read their letters to the whole group. Pass the hat for contributions from those whose Santa letters are the most creative, funniest, most caring—again by choice of the guests.

The evening's second game is somewhat more serious, but with a view toward remembering special Christmases from the past. Ask each guest to complete two statements for the group: "The best gift I ever gave was…" and "The best gift I ever received was…" Pass the hat around again and encourage those whose responses were the most creative or special (as judged by the rest of the guests) to "pay up" and contribute to your worthwhile cause. At the end of the party, quickly tally up all the money in the hat and tell the guests how much they contributed to the charity of your choice.

Limitations and Logistics

The size of your home is the only limitation on this party. Simply gear your guest list to the number, perhaps as few as six or eight, or as many as forty, that will fit into your apartment or house.

Advance preparation is easy. Gather and purchase all kinds of creative supplies with which guests can make hats. Think imaginatively. Provide not only construction paper, markers, scissors, and glue sticks, but also colorful balloons, pipe cleaners, stickers, glitter, toilet paper, Christmas ornaments, and so on. The day of the party, set up one or more large tables—with enough space for guests to work—and put out all your craft materials.

Because guests are each bringing a plate of hors d'oeuvres, you'll only provide hot and cold beverages. Serve the snacks as well as your beverages on a colorful, casual buffet table, using holiday paper goods.

Hats Off to Christmas! Party is a great party idea for couples, singles, and even families as a benefit project.
Hats Off to Christmas! Party was originated by Jan Webb of Phoenix, Arizona.

Chapter 20

Trim the Tree Party

A family event like this one brings everyone closer together. This is an ideal way to entertain a group of singles, especially those who are far from home, with a party that makes them feel like part of the family.

Have the party in your home—or if yours is a growing singles' group, plan the celebration in the church's multipurpose room and enlist the ladies' group to provide all the food and the men's group to donate a large Christmas tree and numerous door prizes. Then get everyone together to share a wonderful meal, decorate a beautiful tree, and spend the evening socializing and singing Christmas carols.

This celebration brings together any group of individuals for the common purpose of enjoying time together and working together to achieve a mutual goal—decorating the most creative and charming tree possible.

Invitation Ideas

Use preprinted invitations, perhaps with a Christmas tree on the front, if you can find them. Or make up a simple flyer on green construction paper or card stock—cut in the shape of a Christmas tree. Print "You are invited to come and trim our tree!" on the front. Provide guests with the usual who, what, when, where, and why—and ask each to dress casually and bring one handmade or purchased ornament. Include an R.S.V.P. and telephone number (for food preparation purposes).

Setting the Mood

Decorations: The tree will be the main decoration for this celebration. Nonetheless, dining tables can be decorated with greenery, flowers, bows, and candles. If the party is in your home, you may also want to adorn the front door, staircase, mantel, and so on.

Music: While recorded Christmas songs and carols are appropriate during dinner, once the meal is over, allow guests to break into Christmas carols—with or without an official song leader and guitarist or pianist.

Enhancements: If your crowd is especially large, decorate two or more trees. Get guests together in teams, decorate each of the trees in different color or ornament schemes, and make decorating a competitive sport.

As guests arrive, greet them warmly with a Christmas-tree-shaped name tag (number them—see below). While this is especially appropriate if your guest list is long and some of your invitees don't know one another, the numbers figure in the evening's entertainment.

Assign guests, especially those who have a hard time mixing, to work together to make simple decorations for the tree such as strings of popcorn and cranberries.

Special Activities

Guests are free to nibble from the Veggie Trees (see end of chapter) before dinner is served. Once the meal is completed, the men—and anyone else interested—can leave immediately to chop down a fresh Christmas tree at a tree farm or to purchase one at a nearby lot. Allow approximately one hour for this activity. (Judge by the proximity of the tree farm or lot you've chosen.) While they're gone, everyone else remaining can complete cleanup and put together popcorn and cranberry strings.

When the tree arrives, it is placed in a stand (add water), and lights are strung (optional). Then, let the decorating begin! Each guest, of course, has the privilege of placing his or her ornament in a special spot on the tree. Encourage everyone to sing carols as they work. It adds to the merriment and spirit of the evening. As decorating nears an end, award door prizes appropriate for either gender from numbers drawn out of a bowl and matched with numbers on guests' name tags.

Theme Variations

If some of the guests will be cutting down a fresh tree and your climate demands it, remind them beforehand to bring along their warmest coats, hats, and gloves.

A single's or women's group may wish to have a Trim the Tree Party with the express purpose of taking the tree to a nursing home or other similar facility. Guests can purchase a small, easily portable tree and trim it with handmade decorations such as painted wooden ornaments, crocheted snowflakes, strings of popcorn, and so on. If time is limited, plan the celebration to include light refreshments instead of a dinner. When the tree is decorated to everyone's satisfaction, transport it in a van to the nursing home. The residents are sure to be delighted with your act of kindness!

Limitations and Logistics

If your party is to be held at home, limit the number of participants to as many as can fit comfortably in the room where you're decorating the tree. If the celebration is held in a larger facility like a church or office meeting room, your guest list can be extended to perhaps one hundred or more. Whichever you choose, the location is not as important as a warm, friendly, "all are welcome" atmosphere.

Once the matter of space is settled, the main limitation is help with the food, especially for a big crowd. If you are coordinating or preparing the food, make it a planned potluck dinner. Assign everyone a simple dish, including the men. (Cheese and crackers or deli slaw don't require any preparation on their part.) Make it a buffet, and decorate a two-sided buffet table with simple greenery, flowers, bows, and candles in festive candle holders. If you don't have enough people to help prepare and serve the food, move the dinner to a restaurant, with participants buying their own meals.

Veggie Trees seem to have been designed for this party. Serve them as predinner nibbles and watch them get untrimmed. (Cover cookie trays with a vegetable dip; construct a Christmas tree shape from celery sticks or green pepper strips; then decorate with cherry tomatoes, cauliflower and broccoli flowerettes, carrot slices, and so on.)

All dinner concerns need to be taken care of ahead of time. You also need to locate the closest Christmas tree farm. If a tree farm is not possible, check out quality and prices at nearby tree lots. Be sure a high-quality tree stand is available and assembled ahead of time. Provide materials for popcorn or cranberry strings, and purchase door prizes appropriate for either gender.

Trim the Tree Party is a good one for couples as well as singles. If you add the reach-out aspect (see Variations), it also is an excellent project for women only!
Donna Christian of Lubbock, Texas, came up with this Trim the Tree Party idea.

Chapter 21

Frosty's Favorite Christmas Party

If you love kids and want to help out some single parents, plan on Frosty's Favorite Christmas Party. This celebration is an especially nice way to bring together singles not only for fun, but also to serve others. Giving their time to benefit others produces a wonderfully satisfying and unifying effect on everyone involved.

Pick a weekend afternoon close to Christmas (so that grateful parents can take a break to finish their Christmas shopping or other preparations without distractions). Wearing their heaviest cold-weather gear, your guests will drive all over town picking up their "borrowed children" (similarly dressed) at the appointed time. When everyone arrives back at your home, send teams (made up of one single and one child) outside to compete in building the best snowman of the afternoon. When the final touches are in place, have a preassigned team of judges inspect the snowmen. Then, herd everyone inside to enjoy caroling and hot chocolate and Christmas cookies, while funny prizes are awarded to every team.

Invitation Ideas

An announcement at your single's group may be the only invitation you need. To make sure that everyone involved has the details, however, you can make up a simple flyer—with snowmen all around the border, of course. Or cut snowman shapes out of white card stock and write out the particulars on each. Make two invitations for each of the singles you invite. (Each uses the second one to invite a young person.)

Give your name and address and the date and time for the party. While an R.S.V.P. is optional, provide your phone number so parents can reach your home if necessary. Be specific about the afternoon's activities so that everyone will know to wear very casual warm clothes, such as jeans, turtlenecks, sweaters, even thermal underwear, plus heaviest coats, boots, mufflers, hats or stocking caps, ski masks, and gloves or mittens—whatever it takes to stay warm when playing in the snow.

Setting the Mood

Decorations: Just focus on what children will think is fun for this celebration. Adorn your Christmas tree with lots of tiny snowmen and colorful ornaments that would especially appeal to children. Use a multitude of snowmen, large and small, all over your party room, and decorate the serving table with snowmen. Make them out of three large marshmallows with tiny plastic top hats and your guests can pop the snowmen (minus hats) into their hot chocolate. Tape large cutout snowmen on windows and walls. (Masking tape works great and will not ruin most wall surfaces if it's not left on too long.) Place a large cardboard cutout snowman on your front door to welcome guests.

Music: Guests may choose to sing carols at any point in the afternoon, but also have some cassettes or compact discs on hand geared to children—songs like "Jingle Bells" and, of course, "Frosty the Snowman"!

Enhancements: A great memento of the afternoon is a photo of teams with their snowmen. Take a roll of film, have double copies made of each print, and send one to each adult and child the week after the party. Or, take Polaroid shots and let children take home their photo the day of the party.

If you want another activity during this gathering, try Right Question, Wrong Answer. To play this game, hand each guest several sheets of paper with pairs of questions you've made up. Some examples:

1. What is one possession that you would like to get rid of?
2. Why do you want to get rid of it?

1. What is your favorite thing to do on a rainy day?
2. Why do you like to do that?

1. What is the first thing you usually say in the morning?
2. Why do you say that?

Have guests write down answers to each pair of questions on a whole page. Have guests keep their first question and answer, and tear off only the answers to the companion questions. Have a large basket or bowl ready for them to place the answers in. One by one, ask guests to re-read their first question and answer. Then, after the companion question is read aloud, they draw one slip out of the basket and read it as a new answer to that question. Wrong answers to right questions! The results are zany and produce loads of laughter.

A creative idea if spoons are to be used for the hot chocolate is to tuck a spoon, even a plastic one, inside an inexpensive mitten. Have each single-and-child team find a matching mitten to make a pair, then send that new pair of mittens home with the child!

Special Activities

When participants arrive, have on hand the standard Frosty decorations: coal for eyes, carrots for noses, hats, and mufflers. (Or ahead of time, instruct singles to bring their own creative set of adornments to use on their snowman.) Set a time limit, perhaps an hour, so young guests won't get frostbite. Give everyone a ten-minute warning, then call time.

Adults help divest children of outerwear, then everyone gathers around a roaring fire—if you have a fireplace. Refreshments and amusing prizes for each child's snowman creativity is next on the agenda. You can also sing familiar carols. As the party closes, double-check to make sure you have each child's wet clothing, prize, and mittens before loading up cars for the trip home.

Theme Variations

Instead of having each single invite a child, make a list of children of single parents who you want to serve, and assign each child to a specific single, preferably in their geographical area of town.

You can plan a different party, but with the same purpose, by also including couples' children.

Limitations and Logistics

The biggest limitation to this party is whether you live in an area where snow is common—indeed, abundant! If you don't, make another party choice.

Decide the maximum number of people your home can hold and divide the number by two. Invite this number of singles, and they'll each invite a child (age eight or above probably works best).

Your main organizational task is arranging transportation to and from the party for the children. Whether each single invites his or her own young friend or you assign a pair, make the single responsible for transporting that child (along with other teams of singles and children, if desired).

Ahead of time, purchase enough small prizes—funny children's gadgets and games— so that each child is awarded one. Make up enough winning categories so that every child receives a prize for some specific aspect of snowman creativity—"Funniest Snowman," "Best Non-Traditional Snowman," "Biggest Snowman," "Smallest Snowman," and so on.

As everyone returns indoors, have some sort of system for storing each individual's wet outerwear, so nothing is left behind at the end of the party. Even a trash bag for each person will do!

Keep food extremely simple. Serve mugs of hot chocolate or cold milk and Christmas cookies—homemade or purchased from a bakery or grocery store. Chips and dip are optional for those rare children who don't like sweets. (Check with parents about food allergies and make note of any. Children aren't always good about avoiding foods they see everyone else eating!) Cover the table with a festive paper or plastic tablecloth and serve the snacks on colorful paper goods for easy cleanup.

Frosty's Favorite Christmas Party is an ideal singles event and a great reach-out project for them.

Chapter 22

Christmas Around the World Party

n a community where there are a great number of people from around the world, plan a Christmas Around the World celebration. Ask everyone—Americans and international guests—to bring a favorite dish from their respective native countries and a small present (from their country) for a gift exchange. Request that those guests who have them, wear traditional costumes from their homelands. As everyone shares their country's customs, native foods, and gifts with one another, the world will seem like a much smaller, friendlier place.

Invitation Ideas

For this celebration, you can use a preprinted invitation with an international look to it. But if you have a long guest list, numerous specific instructions, and a language barrier to overcome, a duplicated flyer—the simpler the better—will work best.

Be sure instructions to the guests are clear and simple. Include your name, the address of the celebration, the date and time of the party, plus an R.S.V.P., and your telephone number—

primarily for answering guests' questions. Also clearly state what each participant should bring. For example, "Please bring eight servings of a dessert that many people from your country enjoy." Also instruct them to bring an item for the international gift exchange that is representative of presents exchanged in their country: "Please bring a small wrapped gift from your homeland that a man or woman would like to receive."

Ask guests to wear a traditional costume or outfit from their country—or region of the United States (cowboy boots and hats for Texans, island dress for Hawaiians, and so on). These costumes should provide excellent conversation starters.

Setting the Mood

Decorations: Make other countries come more alive for your guests by decorating with souvenirs and memorabilia from your own and friends' travels to faraway lands. Adorn the Christmas tree with colorful ornaments from as many countries as possible. Also use cloth or paper flags and dolls dressed in native costumes all over the party room. Place bunches of multicolored balloons (including those with the gift numbers inside) everywhere. Decorate the buffet table with a Christmas or other colorful tablecloth, flowers and greenery, and tiny paper flags from all over the world.

Place a sign on the front door proclaiming "Merry Christmas!" in the language of every country represented at the celebration. These may include:

Brazil/Portugal . . . . *Boas Festas*
China . . . . *Sheng Dan Kuai Le*
C.I.S. (formerly Russia) . . . . *S Rozhdestvom Kristovym*
Finland . . . . *Hauskaa Joulua*
France . . . . *Joyeux Noel*
Germany/Austria . . . . *Frohliche Weihnachten*

Greece . . . . *Kala Christougenna*
Italy . . . . *Buon Natale*
Japan . . . . *Meri Kurisumasu*
Mexico/Spain . . . . *Feliz Navidad*
Netherlands . . . . *Zalig Kerstfeest*
Norway . . . . *Gledelig Jul*
Sweden . . . . *God Jul*

Music: Try to acquire some recorded Christmas music in other languages. Playing these songs as background music during the evening will make guests feel at home and introduce new music to guests from around the world. You can also have several individuals teach the rest of the group a simple Christmas song or carol in their own language. Finally, add a few traditional Christmas carols in English, accompanied by the guitar or piano, to round out the music!

Special Activities

As guests arrive, give them a name tag on which they can write their name and country, plus a stick-on number to put on top of their gifts for placement under the tree.

Start off with this fun icebreaker: As each guest arrives, take him or her away from everyone else and add something unexpected to his or her attire such as a nonfunctional safety pin on a man's cuff, only one earring on a woman, or a bobby pin in a man's hair. After all the guests have arrived, give everyone a blank sheet of paper. Ask each person to greet everyone else at the party and write down, one at a time, each name and what his or her unexpected object is. The game is a sure way of getting to know people you haven't already met. It also produces a lot of laughter and breaks down barriers as guests scrutinize one another!

Dinner can be served next. Arrange all the food on a serving table so guests can sample as many dishes as they wish at this international potluck. As everyone eats, guests can share typical holiday customs from their countries, especially if Christmas is celebrated in their homelands.

After dinner, give each guest a colorful balloon with a number on a square of paper inside. As guests pop their balloons with a hat pin and retrieve the number inside, they match it with the number on a present under the tree and open it. Ask guests to describe or further explain their gift to the group.

Limitations and Logistics

An American home and a friendly, outgoing host or hostess make guests feel welcome to this gathering. Limit the number of guests to six or eight if your house is small. If you have more space, invite as many as two dozen.

Finances should not be a problem since participants will bring most of the food in addition to gifts. The menu will include international dishes and delicacies, coffee, tea, and perhaps milk or punch. To supplement the food offerings, have on hand a large amount of an extra main dish or two such as baked or fried chicken, ham, a casserole, or other similar dish—just in case none of your guests brings an entree.

Place foods and beverages on a simple buffet table by categories—salads, main dishes, desserts, and so on. Have three-by-five-inch cards on hand. As guests place their dishes on the table, they can write both the traditional name of their dishes and their English translations on the cards. Use colorful paper goods for easy cleanup.

Christmas Around the World Party is good for both couples and/or singles.
Kathy Rust, of Durham, North Carolina, introduced me to Christmas Around the World Party.

Chapter 23

Christmas Can Be Nutty! Party

This is a holiday party that certainly isn't the same old Christmas party. It's different—indeed, nutty!

When guests arrive, the only thing edible they'll see are bowls of nuts. Little do they know that they'll be served great food, but have to go through an ingenious scheme to acquire and eat their meal! They'll be given a cryptic menu and told to order three items per course, without any idea of what they are. And they're not allowed to discuss the puzzling menu or the food until the whole nutty dinner is over!

Invitation Ideas

Due to the crazy nature of this party and the smaller number of guests invited, you can simply call and invite each person, informing them of the details over the phone. If you choose to send invitations through the mail, however, keep it simple with only the basic facts. A red or green flyer with nuts and question marks drawn all over it should set the pace! Ask guests to bring a wrapped nutty (gag) gift and, if you wish, ask them to carry the nutty theme further. For example, tell them they must bring or wear some form of nut—peanuts in the shell made into earrings, walnut shell button covers, a small bag of pecans in their pocket, and so on. The wilder their imaginations, the more fun!

Setting the Mood

Decorations: Use nuts everywhere. Serve them in pretty bowls placed all over the party room. Decorate your Christmas tree with miniature nutcrackers and natural ornaments featuring all kinds of nuts in their shells. (Hang them from bright red and green ribbons, using a hot glue gun to attach the two together.) Place a nut wreath on the front door or on a wall in the party room. Pile nuts with the greenery decorating the dining table and have nutcrackers standing sentinel.

Music: Play nutty music. Either songs for holidays other than Christmas—such as July Fourth marches, Valentine's Day love songs, and so on—or funny versions of Christmas songs. (There are an amazing number available, ranging from those by The Chipmunks to a riotous sound of dogs barking out "Silver Bells.")

Enhancements: Award a prize for the "Most Creative Use of Nuts in a Costume." Make the prize— what else—a can of mixed or macadamia nuts!

Special Activities

The main activity of the evening is the Nutty Dinner—the process of serving and enjoying it together. In addition, guests will enjoy participating in a gag gift exchange.

As guests arrive, escort them directly to the dinner table—set only with a tablecloth, a menu, seven three-by-five-inch cards, and a small pencil for each guest. Explain the directions for the meal to all of the guests at the same time:

1. The meal consists of seven courses for each guest. Guests order exactly three items at a time from the menu of twenty-one items.

2. Guests must finish each course (or at least give up the items remaining on their plates) before they can order their next course.

3. Guests may not discuss the food or ask servers or any of the other guests questions about it before the end of the dinner.

This procedure will continue until all guests have ordered, received, and eaten all seven courses. (The end of this chapter provides menu details—although, what the food items really are will not be printed next to their assigned names on the menu.)

After dinner is a potentially lively and laughter-filled time of debriefing about the menu and the food. You can decipher the menu for the guests or the guests can call out their guesses about the foods as you read them aloud.

Afterward, play a nutty game of Pictionary, or Balderdash—a game in which participants make up zany definitions of unknown but actual dictionary words and try to fool the others. Close the evening with a gag gift exchange, white elephant style. (See the White Elephant Party chapter for details.)

Limitations and Logistics

Because serving each guest individually takes quite a bit of time and attention, keep your guest list small—even four or six guests will take a lot of work, so ten to twelve guests may be maximum if you have plenty of help serving.

The main restriction on this party is that you cannot pull it off without quite a bit of help. Share host and/or hostess duties with several different people, or enlist three or four others who are not guests to serve the dinner. Because they will be going back and forth constantly from the kitchen or serving area, filling each guest's plate with their three requested items, each server can cover only two or three guests during dinner.

Your kitchen and serving areas cannot be minute. (A tiny one-person kitchen will not work for this particular gathering.) And although this meal will not be astronomical in cost, you can cut down on your finances if you work with several hosts and/or hostesses and split the costs.

All foods must be completely ready to serve before the dinner begins. For ease in the kitchen, label all twenty-one items clearly with a three-by-five-inch card in front of each.

Christmas Can Be Nutty! Menu

Duplicate the following for each guest, remembering not to clue them in on the dish's true identity:

"The Management has done everything possible to make this an excellent meal. (We assume no responsibility for your health, except to offer ambulance service to the nearest hospital in case of extreme emergency!) Please do not discuss the menu or the food with your server or with any other guest. Select exactly three items per course, write them on a card, and hand them to your server. Please finish each course before you give the server your next order. Enjoy!"

Pay Day (Bread)

Typical Teenager (Nuts)

Shake (Jell-O Salad)

Popeye's Pick (Olive)

Sour Shell (Lemon Meringue Pie)

The Stringers (Green Beans)

Fortune Teller (Tea)

Diamond Chips (Carrots)

Lover's Lane (Spoon)

Pastry Chef (Baked Potato)

Haymaker (Fork)

Last Straw (Toothpick)

Fireworks (Crackers)

Big Engine (V-8)

Sweet Young Thing (Pickles)

Honeymooner's Special (Lettuce Alone)

Cousin Knapp (Napkin)

Funny Actor (Ham)

Guillotine (Knife)

Money Maker (Mint)

Well Known (Ice Water)

Christmas Can Be Nutty! Party is great fun for couples or singles or a mix of the two. Sandra Barnett, of Norman, Oklahoma, combined several ideas she had heard about, gave them a holiday touch, and called the celebration "Christmas Can Be Nutty!"

Chapter 24

Christmas Caroling Hayride

At the holiday season, many people's thoughts turn to traditions of the past. Both a hayride and caroling should evoke fond memories of years gone by. By bringing friends together in a setting of old-fashioned fun, you'll build camaraderie among old friends and new, based on the sheer joy of celebrating the season.

Rent a flatbed with side rails and attach it to a rental or your own truck. Once guests have gathered, take small groups out and about on the side streets of your area to carol for neighbors. Just before they have a chance to get cold, take them back home where they can partake of tasty, hot food while the next group climbs up onto the flatbed for their hayride. As the party concludes, send every guest home with a small gift and attached note, reminding them of the true meaning of Christmas.

Invitation Ideas

Especially if the guest list is extensive, simply duplicate a red or green flyer, glue a piece of straw to it, fold and staple it, and mail it to invitees. Encourage guests to dress casually and layer clothing so they'll be comfortable both indoors and out. An R.S.V.P. and the coordinating hostess's telephone number is optional; add these only if you are concerned about having enough food for a huge crowd.

Setting the Mood

Decorations: Keep them simple—a lovely tree adorned with old-fashioned ornaments, wreaths, garlands, and greenery highlighted with reminders (such as sprigs of hay) of the hayride. If you don't mind the mess, place one or more bales of hay somewhere in the entertaining area to emphasize the hayride theme. They can double for extra chairs! Cover a large table with a casual plastic or paper Christmas tablecloth. Make a centerpiece with an old-fashioned hayride theme or one using hay along with greenery and Christmas flowers.

Music: Guests provide plenty of music as they carol their way through the neighborhood. If you want additional music at home, play old-fashioned Christmas songs and carols as background music.

Enhancements: Send a special "true meaning of Christmas" memento home with your guests. The following are suggestions:

☛ A Christmas cookie cutter with a Bible verse attached

☛ A large candy cane to remind guests of the Good Shepherd and His staff

☛ A small bell with a note to challenge guests to "Let God's love ring through you this year!"

☛ A pine cone covered with birdseed, with the verse, "Look at the birds of the air; they do not sow or reap or store away in barns, and yet your Heavenly Father feeds them. Are you not more valuable than they?"

Special Activities

As guests arrive, the driver can begin loading up those who want to go out first. Or get new people together by handing out numbers as guests arrive (one through six, for example) and encourage them to go on the hayride when their group number is called. Have guests sit back-to-back on the hay bales down the middle of the truck and remind rowdy guests of a few safety rules before you take off. After everyone is seated, the driver can meander through nearby neighborhoods or on not-too-distant country roads with carolers singing all the way. After twenty or thirty minutes, have the driver return home and pick up another group. (Everyone at the gathering has at least one chance to go on the ride. And, at the same time, this prevents guests from getting frostbite in bitter cold climates!)

As guests return to the house, they can place heavy coats, boots, and so on in a designated area and immediately help themselves to the buffet to warm up.

Limitations and Logistics

There are but two limitations to this party. The first is weather; you may not want to invite one hundred people for a specific evening, only to have your party wiped out by a huge blizzard! The second concern is financial. The cost of renting the flatbed, as well as renting a large truck or van to pull it (if you don't own one), in addition to the cost of food, may become prohibitive. An ideal solution to this problem is multiple hosts and hostesses to share the cost, the work, and the fun.

Invite between twenty-five and one hundred people to this gathering. Just be sure to gear your guest list to the size of your entertaining area—the larger the home, the better if you are inviting a multitude. (If you give the party with several other couples, choose the largest house, or at least the largest entertaining area available, among them so that you can invite as many guests as you wish and still have plenty of room for celebrating.)

Preparty preparation includes:

☞ **Flatbed and truck:** Several weeks in advance, make all reservations for the flatbed, the truck or van to pull it, and a generator for lighting on it. String lights overhead down the length of the flatbed and secure to poles at both ends. Secure six or so hay bales, depending on the size of your flatbed. They can be purchased at a feed store or stable and generally sold back to the same establishment for about one-half the price after you've used them. A good configuration is four bales lengthwise down the center of the flatbed and one crosswise at each end—in the shape of a long "I". Take the flatbed and truck on a trial run before taking out guests!

☞ **Neighbors:** Prepare and duplicate simple flyers to let neighbors know that you will be caroling on the given date. Also check with local authorities to see if you need any kind of permit to drive the truck through your area.

☞ **Song sheets:** Duplicate and staple together simple song sheets with verses to familiar Christmas carols.

☞ **Food:** The one essential characteristic for the evening's food is that it be hot. Make it available to chilled carolers throughout the evening, since guests will be coming in and going out. Serve everything buffet-style using colorful paper and plastic ware so guests can dispose of them whenever they finish eating. (Have large visible trash containers available.)

Perhaps serve a Caroler's menu—all starting with the letter "C"— such as chicken corn chowder or chili, carrot strips (and other raw vegetables), cheese and crackers, Christmas cookies, cocoa, cider (hot or cold), and coffee.

Christmas Caroling Hayride is a super party for couples, singles, families, or as an office party. Jim and Donna Warren, of Huntington Beach, California, started their annual Christmas Caroling Hayride eight years ago.

Chapter 25

Semiformal Christmas Dinner Party

ingles love to get together and party. Any holiday or occasion will do! Pull out all the stops and really celebrate the season with a Semiformal Christmas Dinner. Get together a few friends to attend to every little detail, and it will be an extraordinarily festive way to celebrate the holidays.

Invitation Ideas

Personalized, handcrafted invitations are extremely nice for this special party. Use high-quality paper or card stock (available from stationers, art supply stores, and printers). Write out the details in calligraphy, perhaps in dark red or green ink. Add Christmas ribbons, glitter, and whatever else you choose to make them look elegant.

If your time is limited, choose formal-looking commercial invitations and fill in all the details. For either choice, an R.S.V.P. is a necessity (with a telephone number), as is a note about dress. Although "black tie" (tuxedos for the men, and formals for the ladies) is not necessary, you may want to define semiformal on the invitations, stating, "Suit and tie for the men, dressy evening wear for the ladies."

Also ask guests to bring a high-quality wrapped gift. Men should bring a man's gift, women a gift for another woman. (Put a generous price limit on the gifts, perhaps fifteen to twenty dollars, if you feel that guests can afford it.)

Setting the mood

Decorations: Everything about the decorations for this celebration should be festive and beautiful. Choosing a unique color scheme will go a long way in guiding your selections. The possibilities are endless, but you might try burgundy and silver, or blue, green, and gold. The dinner tables will set a lovely stage for the rest of your decorating.

Create a stunning Christmas tree—perhaps exclusively decorated in the two or three colors you've chosen—of bows, ornaments, and lights. Accent wreaths, fireplace mantel, and stair rails with garlands of greenery, lights, and decorations of the same colors. Place glowing candles all over the house and leave potpourri simmering on the stove throughout the evening. Be sure to place a beautiful wreath on the front door to welcome your guests.

The meal is a sit-down dinner, complete with festive place cards, fine china, and crystal. Use Christmas plaid tablecloths and solid-colored runners—with solid white china for a dramatic effect—or choose solid-colored tablecloths and plaid runners with any pattern of fine china. Use lots of festive candles on each table, plus Christmas flower arrangements (which make nice take-home gifts for the women).

Music: Lovely recorded Christmas songs and carols of an instrumental nature provide just the right background music. Guests also may choose to sing a few traditional carols at a designated time during the evening.

Enhancements: During a given time period, individuals, couples, or small groups can slip away to a designated area, perhaps in front of the Christmas tree or decorated fireplace, to have their pictures taken. These photos later serve as a lovely reminder of an elegant evening together with friends.

Special Activities

As guests arrive, take their wraps and the gift they've brought. Give each a name tag cut in the shape of a Christmas ornament. Place men's gifts on one side of the Christmas tree; ladies' on the opposite side. Early arriving guests can help themselves to a cup of eggnog or hot wassail. Once the last guests arrive, dinner can be announced and served.

Immediately after dessert, have guests move into the room where they'll be for the rest of the evening—preferably a room with a Christmas tree and, perhaps, a fireplace. After guests are comfortably seated, ask a designated singer or pianist to lead everyone in singing a few Christmas carols. Next, someone can read a moving Christmas story. (Go to your local library and choose one from the *Reader's Digest Christmas Storybook*, *Guideposts*, or another similar publication.) Afterward, one by one, ask guests to share a favorite Christmas memory or tradition with the group. Guests may help themselves again, at this point, to a hot or cold beverage. If time permits, a host or hostess can also read the Christmas story from Luke 2.

Finally, have guests draw a number out of a bowl or festive basket to determine in what order they will choose a gift from under the tree on respective sides.

Limitations and Logistics

An even number of guests, with an equal number of men and women, is ideal for this party—perhaps twelve to twenty-four people, if space allows. The best location is a home large enough to comfortably welcome all your guests.

The primary limitations on this celebration may be your time and expenses. In either case, sharing responsibilities with friends can work in your favor. If time is at a premium, carefully think through shortcuts you can take concerning the food, invitations, and so on. If cost is the main restriction, cut back—divide all the shopping, cooking, and serving duties among the host group. If cost is not a factor, have the party catered, and hire a professional photographer, cutting down on the workload tremendously.

Preparation for all aspects of the evening should be completed well in advance so that you can fully enjoy yourself with the guests. Advance work can include: planning a traditional, sumptuous menu and securing a good caterer or preparing all of the food and beverages; securing a good professional photographer, setting his or her hours, and choosing special decorations for the area where pictures will be taken; decorating and setting guest tables; planning a special Christmas reading; and thinking through a sharing time in which guests can participate.

Plates should be served from the kitchen. Unless the party is catered, this will probably involve all of the hosts or hostesses at serving and clearing times.

Semiformal Christmas Dinner Party is ideal for singles and also makes a special office party.
Brenda Barnett of Houston, Texas, pulled out all the stops with this one when she was single.

Chapter 26

Ladies Night Out Christmas Party

What do all the young mothers you know need desperately? A night out! So turn your own need for a night out on the town into a plan for a Ladies Night Out Christmas Party.

Invite friends to dress up and meet at a trendy restaurant for dinner. After a leisurely meal, have everyone return to your home to continue the festivities. Exchange gifts and organize a creative conversation game. Because there are no children allowed—no spilled milk to clean up, no runny noses to wipe, and no fights to referee—the evening will be a much-needed time of relaxation and renewing of friendships with one another. It will be midnight before you know it!

Invitation Ideas

Choose a festive feminine preprinted invitation for this event! Fill in the location and address of the restaurant as well as your home address. Since some friends may only be able to participate in a portion of the celebration, include the time guests are to arrive at the restaurant as well as an estimated time of return to your home. Add an R.S.V.P. and your telephone number. Ask guests to bring a wrapped gift of a specific nature, in a given price range—or set a theme where pampering is the focus, and suggest such items as a certificate for a facial or a manicure or special bath products.

Add a word about how to dress. You know your friends well enough to know whether they'd prefer to get out their "best" or opt for very casual but festive outfits.

Setting the Mood

Decorations: Use traditional or old-fashioned ornaments to decorate your Christmas tree in a color scheme that is extended throughout the party room. Decorate both the mantel and indoor wreaths with satin or velveteen bows and ornaments in the same color. Light lots of candles, too. Try wrapping all your pictures in festive Christmas wrap and bows and rehanging them on your walls. Place your prettiest Christmas wreath (or make one adding silk flowers and ornaments in your chosen color) to welcome guests as they come in your front door.

Music: Aim for a relaxing mood. Play Christmas songs and carols softly in the background.

Special Activities

The primary activity of the evening (after dinner together at a nice restaurant) is the enjoyment of exchanging adult conversation, as well as gifts.

After the women arrive at the restaurant and are shown to the room you've reserved, each guest orders from the menu, enjoys a leisurely meal, and pays her own bill. Afterward, everyone returns to your home. (You may want to leave a few minutes early to get home and be ready to welcome the guests.)

After you take her coat, have each woman draw a number out of a lovely crystal bowl. Use these numbers to determine the order for choosing a gift from under the tree. You can conduct this like a white elephant gift exchange, in which guests choose a wrapped gift or "steal" an already opened one from an earlier participant. (See the White Elephant Christmas Party chapter for details.) Since gifts have been carefully chosen, however, you might forgo this element of the exchange.

The final organized activity of the evening involves planned conversations. To create a lively discussion, choose one or more of the following topics, and give each woman a chance to answer:

- **If I had a million dollars, I would …**
- **Someday I want to write a book about …**
- **The most bizarre thing in my purse tonight is …**
- **Don't tell anyone, but my favorite food is …**
- **My most embarrassing moment was …**
- **The most important thing or person in my life is …**

Guests can help themselves to a beverage at any time during this final half of the evening.

Theme Variations

If finances are not of significant concern, invite a somewhat limited number of women to this celebration and take care of the restaurant bill for everyone. Remember, however, this is not necessary—most women are so happy to have a night out that they won't mind covering the cost of their own dinner!

Limitations and Logistics

Invite any number of women, from four to twenty-four; just be sure there is comfortable seating for everyone you're inviting. If the restaurant that you choose provides a wide range of prices, finances will not be a restriction for any of your guests.

Your preparation is minimal: Make dinner reservations at a special restaurant, preferably in a private room; plan out the gift exchange; and prepare a hot beverage and some Christmas cookies to serve to guests. If the crowd is small, put refreshments out on the coffee table. For a larger group, set up a pretty buffet table covered with a lovely linen tablecloth and decorated with a Christmas floral arrangement as a centerpiece. Whichever way, use good china cups and saucers, and put out an assortment of flavored hot teas and a pretty teapot full of hot water.

Ladies Night Out Christmas Party is just for the ladies!
Suzanne Frank of Irvine, California, came up with this women-pleasing idea.

Chapter 27

Christmas Cookie Decorating Party

We all love Christmas, and some of us even enjoy the cooking that goes along with the holidays. But let's be practical: we sometimes need encouragement to get going on our Christmas baking.

So, why not bake dozens and dozens and dozens of cookies from a favorite sugar cookie recipe and freeze them? Then, send out invitations, defrost the cookies, and set up a number of decorating stations. At the end of your party, guests will be delighted to take home several dozen personally decorated cookies for family and friends.

Invitation Ideas

For this gathering, invitations can be preprinted and informal or a simple cutout, using construction paper or card stock and tracing around a cookie cutter. Include your name and address, the date and time (this makes a great afternoon party), and a note to bring an apron since cookie decorating can get pretty messy! If you wish, ask each guest to bring a specific amount and type of cookie decoration.

For instance, "Please bring two large packages of red and green peanut M & Ms." An R.S.V.P. and hostess's phone number is optional.

Setting the Mood

Decorations: If time allows, decorate some of the cookies ahead of time, attach a ribbon through a hole (baked into each cookie at the top), and use these and other colorful ornaments to decorate your Christmas tree. Also hang decorated cookies from bright ribbons in the center of kitchen windows. For the front door, attach sturdy, decorated cookies securely to a wreath of greenery. As your guests arrive, it will say to them, "Welcome! Come in and be creative!"

Music: Guests may choose to sing familiar Christmas carols and songs as they work. Wonderful! Or, if desired, play recorded Christmas music in the background, throughout the celebration.

Special Activities

Invite everyone to take a spot at one of the decorating stations. To keep her completed cookies separate, each woman can put them on sturdy paper plates on the "finished" table with a three-by-five-inch card with her name written on it. (Guests will also know who to compliment as they admire everyone else's masterpieces!) Supply rolls of cellophane (or foil) and colorful ribbons to cover plates for transportation home. Invite women to help themselves to simple refreshments at any time.

Lots of good conversation rounds out this creative celebration. If you wish, use selected cookie cutters to share the Christmas story with your guests. (See the end of this chapter for details.)

Theme Variations

Involve guests in the cookie-making process earlier, if you wish. Provide chilled dough and set your friends loose with cookie cutters. Keep in mind, however, that this takes quite a bit more time—and careful attention—than decorating already-baked cookies.

You can also make gingerbread men or use another type of dough for different kinds of cookies. Regardless of what you use, the actual decorating of the cookies is what makes this party such a fun exercise in creativity!

This party also makes an excellent mother-daughter activity.

Limitations and Logistics

Depending on the size of your kitchen and adjoining work areas (and your intestinal fortitude with regard to how many dozen cookies you can bake), eight to twelve might be an ideal number of friends to invite to this party. Your home is the best location for this party, although a rented facility with a kitchen will work, so long as numerous tables, chairs, and the correct utensils are available.

Space is probably the only real restriction to this event. While a tiny apartment with a one-person kitchen probably will not work, even a house with a modest kitchen can be supplemented with folding tables. If you use card tables as your decorating stations, invite women in multiples of four to keep seating just right. (Do try to confine all your work to noncarpeted areas.)

If supplying a multitude of cookie decorations in addition to frosting and cookies for the whole crowd is too expensive, share hostessing with a friend or two. Or, ask each guest to bring a sizable quantity of one single type of cookie decoration to share with the whole group. (See list below for suggestions.)

Ahead of time, using all the cookie cutter shapes you have available, bake about two dozen cookies per guest. Store prebaked cookies in airtight containers and freeze for up to one month. Defrost them the morning of the party.

Also prepare and tint enough icing to put five to eight colors at each decorating station. White, red, and green are absolutely necessary and will require the largest batches. Other possibilities are yellow, blue, orange, brown (chocolate), and black (licorice). Recycle plastic food containers and dispose of them when the party is over. Fill each with one color of icing for every station. Place a small plastic knife in each bowl. (You can also fill pastry bags with various colors of icing and supply a variety of decorating tips.) In addition, place some of each type of decoration at every station. Suggestions are as follows:

- Nuts
- Silver candy balls
- Candy mints or wafers
- Red hots
- Multicolored sprinkles
- Shredded coconut

- M & Ms
- Crushed candy canes
- Life Savers
- Small jelly beans
- Hershey Kisses
- Raisins

- Colored sugars
- Peppermint candies
- Mini marshmallows
- Gumdrops

You can't just throw away those broken cookies…so put them out for taste testing—along with a simple buffet of nonsweet snacks, frosty cold mugs of milk, and hot coffee. Focus on healthy foods since the sugar content at this party is approaching overload! Cover the buffet table simply (even pretty paper is fine), and use a decorative Christmas cookie jar surrounded by greenery as a centerpiece. Food might include whole-wheat crackers and cheeses, crudités with shrimp or onion dip, and gourmet chips.

Christmas Cookie Cutters

This narrative of the Christmas story comes via the ministry of Emilie Barnes. Several women she knows have put together these Christ-Centered Cookie Cutter Creations. For more details or to order a set of six Christmas cookie cutters, along with a recipe for whole-wheat cookies, for $5.75, contact:

> More Hours in My Day
> 2838 Rumsey Drive
> Riverside, California 92506
> 909-682-4714

Use your cookie cutters by holding up each shape and saying:

1. (Christmas Tree) Here's a Christmas tree. Do you like Christmas? I love it! What goes under our trees? Presents. I love presents, too! Let's talk about who received the very first Christmas presents.

2. (Angel) There were three very wise men. An angel came to them, told them to look up in the sky, and they saw a star.

3. (Star) The angel told the three wise men to follow the star. When they did, it took them to Bethlehem where they found our Lord. They gave Him their gifts: a bag of gold, a jar of frankincense—a perfume of flowers similar to potpourri—and a special box of myrrh, the perfume of spices.

4. (Heart) The heart represents love. Don't we all think of love when we see a heart? Do you know that God loves you? He loved you so much that He gave you a sacrificial gift, His Son, Jesus Christ. Sacrificial? Yes, something that is very precious, but you give it away.

5. (Cross) The cross represents life. The cross represents Jesus, the reason for the season. The baby Jesus grew up. He learned to walk and talk, and became a man. He went to the cross and died for our sins—past, present, and future. When we believe in Him,

He forgives us our sins and gives us eternal life. It never ends; it goes on forever and ever, eternally. When Jesus died, He went to Heaven to be with His Father, but He left the Holy Spirit with us.

6. (Dove) The dove represents God's Holy Spirit. The Spirit of Jesus lives within us when we believe and receive Him into our hearts, which means that we are never alone. God is always with us, to love and comfort us.

7. (Church) The church represents worship. What do we do in church? We sing, hear God's Word from the Bible, pray, and worship God. Church is a very important time in our week. It is also a place where we can bring friends to hear about Christ and to experience fellowship with one another.

8. (Candle) The candle represents light. Matthew 5:16 says that we are to let our light shine. Our faith, our thoughts, and our feelings are to be full of light. Light gives a welcome feeling. Christmas gives us a special opportunity to let our light shine. We can tell others about Jesus, and that we celebrate His birth on Christmas.

Christmas Cookie Decorating Party is ideal for a women-only party or as a family activity for mothers and daughters.

Chapter 28

Christmas Brunch and Ornament Exchange

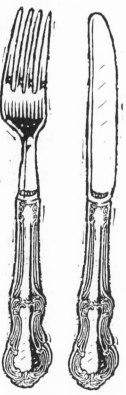

While an ornament exchange certainly isn't a new idea, if you add a brunch and mix in a white-elephant-style gift exchange, it's a winning combination! So, invite your friends and start ornament shopping!

Invitation Ideas

Make ornament-shaped cutouts from card stock or shop for preprinted invitations in this shape or with ornaments printed on them.

Tell your guests the party will feature an ornament exchange and ask them to wrap the ornaments as gifts. Specify a price range. In addition to the usual information, suggest casual guest attire unless you think guests will welcome the opportunity to get dressed up. Add an R.S.V.P. and your telephone number so that you'll have an accurate count for food preparation.

Setting the Mood

Decorations: Ornaments, ornaments, and more ornaments are called for! Adorn your tree, add them to garlands and other greenery, and hang them from ribbons in windows. Make a collage of cards that feature beautiful ornaments. Greet guests with a wreath on your door that's chock-full of small ornaments. For your buffet table, decorate a small tree with tiny exquisite ornaments as the centerpiece and, with ribbon, tie ornaments around linen napkins.

Music: Play recorded Christmas songs and carols as quiet background music.

Enhancements: If you tie ornaments around linen napkins, invite guests to take those ornaments home, too.

Special Activities

If you wish—and if many guests do not know one another—provide festive name tags in the shape of ornaments as guests arrive. Direct guests to place their wrapped ornament under the tree, find a chair, and join others in conversation. As soon as everyone has arrived, serve brunch, inviting everyone to help themselves from your sumptuous buffet table.

Then, begin the ornament exchange with a modified white elephant exchange by drawing one name at a time out of a bowl or pretty basket. After the first name is called and the guest has chosen a wrapped ornament from under the tree, subsequent guests choose a wrapped gift or "steal" one already opened (up to three times only). Draw names until everyone has an ornament, then, if guests wish, they can trade ornaments to their hearts' content.

Theme Variations

☞ Request that guests bring an ornament they've made themselves.

☞ If finances are not a concern, treat guests to brunch at a restaurant and carry on the ornament exchange at your home. (Or arrange for everyone to meet at a restaurant, pay for their own meal, and then hold the ornament exchange at your home.)

☞ Forgo the buffet, and plan a sit-down brunch.

☞ Instead of an ornament exchange, make it an ornament shower for a bride-to-be or newly married couple. As each ornament is unwrapped, it can be placed on a small tree—the new couple's first tree together.

Limitations and Logistics

Your only restrictions may be on the cost and time needed to prepare a fairly elaborate brunch. If you have the party at home, consider teaming up with a friend to share expenses and food preparation. (If cost is not a concern, have the brunch catered and really enjoy the party!)

Additional preparty planning tips are as follows:

☞ Cook and freeze food items up to two weeks in advance.

☞ Be sure you have adequate seating and places to perch plates so everyone is comfortable.

☞ Purchase and wrap a few extra ornaments in case someone forgets theirs or an ornament gets broken.

Serve this brunch on sturdy festive paper goods—or better yet, on china. Plan your menu around dishes that can be prepared ahead of time. Some suggestions are as follows: spiced fruit compote, cheese custard, hot Canadian bacon slices, red and green endive salad with raspberry vinaigrette dressing, assorted fruit breads and flavored butters, juice, coffee, and tea.

Christmas Brunch and Ornament Exchange is a great way to get together with women friends or as a ladies' office party.

Chapter 29

Santa's Workshop Party

Let's face it, many of us put off wrapping Christmas gifts until a day or two before the event. Rather than bemoan the fact, turn it into a Santa's Workshop Party.

Invite like-minded friends to come to your home a few days before Christmas. Have your unwrapped gifts and wrapping materials on hand—paper, ribbon, tags, tape, and decorations. Ask guests to dress casually and bring ten gifts or more for wrapping, plus additional wrapping materials to share. Set up card tables in several adjoining rooms, provide a few simple snacks, and you've got a party.

Everyone wins! No new Christmas outfits. No fancy desserts to make. No gift exchange. Just good fellowship, and everyone goes home with armloads of beautifully wrapped gifts and the satisfaction that they're almost caught up on Christmas.

Invitation Ideas

It is perfectly acceptable to invite other women to this gathering with a simple phone call. If you decide on a flyer instead, just type or write out the details on a sheet of white paper and duplicate it on green or red. In addition to the usual details, ask guests to dress casually, jeans if they wish, and "Bring several rolls of Christmas wrapping and ribbon to share with others." An R.S.V.P. and telephone number are unnecessary unless you're inviting so many friends that you are concerned about having enough work tables.

Setting the Mood

Decorations: This is a work party, after all! Don't do anything extra. (Besides, since this party is held just before Christmas, your house will probably already be decorated.)

Music: Christmas songs and carols are appropriate for background music. Encourage everyone to sing along!

Enhancements: Provide large cardboard boxes (get them free at grocery stores) or clean trash bags in which guests carry home their beautifully wrapped gifts.

Special Activities

As guests arrive, invite them to settle in at tables (perhaps two women at each card table and three to five at larger tables). Each guest may keep some of her gift wrap, ribbons, and tags at her table and place the rest at a "wrapping center" for all the guests to share. Guests can go to work as soon as they are set up. Suggest they place their unwrapped gifts underneath and beside their wrapping area. Be sure to have tape and sharp scissors at each wrapping table. As you begin, the hostess may want to remind everyone to put a tag on every gift they wrap; who among us hasn't wrapped a beautiful gift, only to forget what's in it and who it's for? Encourage the women to help themselves to simple snacks and a beverage any time they wish.

Here is an idea for gifts that must be mailed or shipped: Save your Christmas cards each year, and (after you've read them a second time) cut off the decorative front from the prettiest ones. Match cards with wrapping paper and use double-stick tape to adhere them to the front of packages. Voila! Personalized wrapped gifts arriving at their destinations without crushed bows!

Limitations and Logistics

Any number of guests is fine for this party. Six is not too few and twenty is not too many. The only restriction to this gathering is space. If it is limited, make use of dining room and kitchen tables, and move sofas and other large pieces of furniture against the walls to make room for additional tables.

The preparation for Santa's Workshop is simple. Secure enough card tables or larger tables to accommodate all of your guests. You also need to provide sharp scissors (or ask them to bring their own) and tape for everyone. You also may want to supply kraft paper and clear carton sealing tape for guests who must mail gifts out of town. Finally, prepare a very simple snack for guests to munch on as they work.

Limit food to no-frills finger foods served on holiday paper goods. Use a disposable tablecloth. If you want a centerpiece, pile up several colorful gifts that are already wrapped.

Santa's Workshop Party is a great fellowship time for "women only."
Laura Quay of Irvine, California, suggested Santa's Workshop Party.

Chapter 30

Christmas Friendship Party

If you're new in town (or know someone who is new and longs for an opportunity to get to know some other women), throw a Christmas Friendship Party. Invite the wives of your husband's new business associates to join you. In addition, ask each woman to bring along one of her own friends you have not met.

Gather in your home or a lovely room of your church. Share a meal together and spend a delightful evening getting to know new friends. You'll find each guest will be appreciative of the opportunity to be part of such a gathering of wonderful new friends.

Invitation Ideas

Purchase pretty preprinted invitations for this party. (See if you can find one with a "join the group" theme.) Include your name and the address of the party location, the date and time, and suggestions on how to dress. Festive but casual dress is ideal for this party. Add an R.S.V.P. and your telephone number. Be sure to explain the purpose of the party. Enclose a second invitation to remind each guest that she is expected to bring a friend you haven't met or another woman who is new to town. (Leave their envelopes blank.) By this process, at least half of the guests probably will not have met one another. New friendships!

Setting the Mood

Decorations: Set up the buffet table with a pretty tablecloth in Christmas colors or another color scheme. Use dolls in festive dresses as a centerpiece—placing them close together as if they are holding hands. Decorate your tree with tiny dolls, too. Use red and white hearts liberally on the tree and on wreaths, and adorn the mantel with greenery, hearts, and more small dolls. Be sure to light a roaring fire if you have a fireplace. Finally, place a beautiful wreath on your front door. Decorate it with small dolls and a banner reading: "Welcome to all new friends!"

Music: Christmas songs or carols played softly in the background is all you need. Be sure music is low enough so as to not detract from conversations.

Enhancements: Ask women to "sign in" with their name, address, and telephone number on a prepared sheet or in a blank book. The week after the party, type up the list and mail it to everyone who was present.

Special Activities

Activities all revolve around building friendships. As guests arrive, greet them warmly and give each a name tag cut from card stock or construction paper like two paper dolls with hands connected. These name tags are designed to make connections in other guests' minds. *Your* guest's name tag will display *her* name on the left doll and "I brought [the name of *her* guest]" on the right doll. *Her* guest's name tag will have *her* name on the left doll and "I came with [the name of *your* guest]" on the right doll.

After everyone has arrived, invite guests to go through a buffet line and be seated at tables of four to eight—in order to eat in a more intimate setting. Ask guests to go out of their way to get to know every other woman at her table. After dinner, guests move into another area and sit in a large circle to get involved in relational activities. Choose one or more of the following exercises to better acquaint guests:

- **Pocketbook Treasures:** Each guest empties her purse into her own lap. Vote and award a prize for the most bizarre contents.
- **Team Charades:** Play charades with a theme: famous women or cartoon characters, for example.
- **Christmas Couplets:** Each guest must make up a couplet related to Christmas and recite it to the group.
- **Skits:** Break up into teams which perform a three-minute spoof of a nursery rhyme, television show, or other category.
- **Twenty Questions:** Teams of four to eight try to come up with the answers to prepared questions about politics, gourmet cooking, sports, the Bible, foreign countries, or trivia. Award prizes to members of the winning team.
- **Name That Celebrity:** Break up into teams. Every guest places five to ten celebrity names—from all walks of life—on slips of paper and places these in a basket, to be drawn out one at a time. Teams try to guess who their own team member is trying to describe by using only hints or clues. Teams guess as many correct names as possible in sixty seconds. Award prizes to winning team members.

As these activities are completed, guests can mingle with another beverage in hand.

Theme Variations

If you and a few friends have prepared the food for this celebration in lieu of having it catered, ask husbands to be the waiters for this party. (They may want to wear black slacks, white shirts, and red or black bow ties to serve!) One other fun twist: Encourage husbands (ahead of time) to prepare and present a brief skit, such as a modern reenactment of Dickens's *A Christmas Carol*. If they agree to it, the results should be hilarious!

Limitations and Logistics

Eight to twelve guests may be just right for your home, but you may wish to invite as many as twenty or more. Even though a home will provide the most warmth, a nicely decorated church, business meeting room, or private room in a restaurant will be very adequate for a larger group. Create your own atmosphere of graciousness and out-of-the-ordinary hospitality!

If this celebration is held in a rented facility or as a catered event, finances may pose a problem. You can solve both of these dilemmas easily, however. Have the party in your home, even if that means restricting your guest list, and prepare a simple meal, hors d'oeuvres or a dessert instead of hiring a caterer.

If you decide to prepare the food, share hostessing duties with a friend and divide the work in half! Consider an easy approach: a Waffle Bar lunch buffet, for example, with multiple toppings such as assorted fruit, flavored butters and syrups, chopped nuts, and whipped cream, with coffee and tea. For dinner, try a Baked Potato Bar with multiple toppings: butter, sour cream, grated cheeses, crumbled bacon or seasoned ground beef, and chives, with punch or coffee. Pass around a plate of Christmas cookies for dessert. Serve guests on china or festive paper goods.

Christmas Friendship Party is a great "for women only" idea.
Mary Di Rienzo came up with the idea for a Christmas Friendship Party several years ago when she was new to St. Louis, Missouri.

Chapter 31

Christmas Tea Party

S tage a lovely afternoon tea for the women in your family or your family of friends. It's a wonderful way to honor members of your extended family during the holiday season, and some may look forward to your tea as "the calm before the storm!"

Have guests dress in their Sunday best to enjoy a few peaceful hours of chitchat, catching up with family and friends. Serve traditional tea-and-crumpet-style refreshments. Invite all the women you really care about—from a broad spectrum of ages (late teens to their late seventies or eighties). The conversation is sure to be lively and heartwarming for everyone!

Invitation Ideas

Find preprinted invitations for a Christmas tea, if you can. Send them out in mid-November for an early December date, before the holiday rush. This way everyone can look forward to a relaxing afternoon for several weeks. In addition to the expected information, add an R.S.V.P. and your telephone number. Encourage the women to dress up.

(This is not a "jeans and tennis shoes" affair!) Set up two simple rules for this gathering: No children or babies allowed. Don't bring anything but yourself (unless you offer Great Aunt Fannie a ride)! These rules alone should make your guests wild with anticipation!

Setting the Mood

Decorations: Festive is the byword! Everything you can do to make guests feel welcome, cheerful, and ready for the holidays is wonderful. Simmer potpourri on the stove throughout the afternoon. A roaring fire is a must if you have a fireplace. Light candles everywhere, even in the guest bathroom! Place several crèches in prominent places around the party room, and decorate your Christmas tree early—perhaps in colors this year that will especially appeal to women. Also adorn the mantel, staircase, and other focal points, and put your most elaborate wreath or arrangement on the front door to tell each woman, from the moment she arrives, "You are special!"

Music: The best musical touch to add to this celebration is relaxing, beautiful Christmas melodies played softly in the background—so softly they are barely noticeable.

Enhancements: Ask each guest to bring a special wrapped ornament for an exchange. Or, give out small mementos of the afternoon together such as a small Christmas ornament, a meaningful note, or a small book that's a reminder to guests of the true meaning of Christmas.

Special Activities

As women arrive, offer them a warm beverage and show them to the party room. Comfortable chairs should be arranged in a broad circle or a horseshoe shape. Women don't ever seem to have a problem finding things to talk about! But if there are guests who are unusually shy or quiet, ask a few other guests to engage these women in conversation.

Perhaps halfway through the afternoon, invite your guests to join you for delicate refreshments. Guests can help themselves from an assortment of hot beverages and a beautifully set buffet. Everyone can return to their chairs and eat as conversation continues. If you wish, read the Christmas story from Luke 2 or another devotional reading during this time.

Limitations and Logistics

Include all of your local female relatives and/or any special group of women in this gathering. The exact size of the group is not as critical as having a chair for each woman. If the size of your entertaining area is restrictive, pull the chairs closer together; no one will mind a bit!

Your primary limitation may be time. You'll have to make time to decorate your home early in the season in order to be ahead of the Christmas rush. And you'll probably want to cook, bake, and freeze food items a few weeks in advance so everything is prepared for the tea. (Having completed both of these tasks, you will be far more ready to enjoy the tea— and the entire holiday season—than virtually anyone you know!) You can cut down on your time investment by using a good bakery and the services of other food specialists.

Make the refreshments at this tea extra special. Of course, serve your guests on your finest china. Be creative and arrange a hot beverage bar. Serve gourmet coffees and hot teas with a multitude of choices for toppings: whipped cream, mini chocolate chips, powdered cinnamon and cinnamon sticks, peppermint candy cane stirrers, colored sugars, chocolate shavings or sprinkles, and so on. Provide flavored nondairy creamers, if you like—Irish cream, amaretto, and others. This elegant layout alone will make guests feel like ladies, not like the usual cook, laundress, chauffeur, and maid!

On a separate table, serve an assortment of "high tea" foods on matching china. Use your favorite family recipes or frozen gourmet items such as Quiche Lorraine, as well as baked goods from an excellent bakery. And, of course, your menu will include the season's first Christmas cookies.

Adorn both serving tables with your prettiest linens and best silver, china, crystal, and serving trays and platters. (Just a linen napkin along with the refreshments will make each guest feel special.) Christmas flower arrangements make simple, elegant centerpieces.

Christmas Tea Party is great for women family and friends, or plan it as a party for female office friends.
Kim Brandt of Irvine, California, gave me this lovely Christmas Tea Party idea.

Chapter 32

Christmas Craft
and Dessert Party

f crafts and fellowship are activities you and your friends love, this party is for you. Invite friends over early in December and provide all the supplies to make unique Christmas decorations. By the time the evening is over, you and your guests not only will have beautiful, professional-looking crafts, but also the warm feeling of fellowship not unlike that of an old-fashioned quilting bee.

Invitation Ideas

Although you can use simple Christmas note cards for invitations, this is the perfect party to show off your own handcrafting skills. You might make festive fold-overs on white card stock with sprigs of holly and small bows glued on, and write on them using red or green ink.

Tell your guests it will be a craft-making party and they will be making their own ornaments. Suggest guests dress casually and bring an apron to protect their clothes. Provide your telephone number, and stress the need for an R.S.V.P. For example, "Please R.S.V.P. by December 2, so I will have enough craft materials on hand for everyone." (If the project you plan requires a hot glue gun, add a note to request that guests who have one bring it along to share.)

Setting the Mood

Decorations: Use as much in the way of handcrafted ornaments as possible. Adorn your tree with them and add them to garlands and other greenery. Display a handcrafted manger scene in a prominent spot and display handmade quilts and other projects. Your buffet table centerpiece might be a small tree with minuscule handmade ornaments. And greet guests at the front door with a wreath of your own design!

Music: As guests work on their projects, play recorded Christmas songs and carols as background music.

Enhancements: During dessert, ask guests to share with the group some thoughts about how the craft projects they have just completed relates to the spirit of Christmas.

Send guests home with a booklet of devotional thoughts for the Christmas season, in addition to their new lovely Christmas decoration.

Special Activities

As guests arrive, invite them to help themselves to a beverage and choose the supplies they need to complete their craft project. Ask them to take a seat at an open spot at one of the tables and start to work. Everyone works at a different speed, so as guests' crafts are complete, invite them to help themselves to dessert or a beverage. Quick finishers may wish to wander around and look at others' work. As everyone completes their work, guests can all retire to another room with their dessert and beverage. If you wish, you can read aloud the Christmas story from Luke 2 during this time.

Limitations and Logistics

If you have the party at home, the size of the room in which you choose to do the crafts will limit the number of guests—although even a basement room with long tables set up is appropriate. The only other restriction might be a financial one. If craft supplies for everyone are out of the range of your budget, ask guests to supply their own unfinished ornament or ask friends to share in the hostessing expenses.

Some preparty planning tips are as follows:

☛ Choose a craft project that can be completed during the time allowed for your party.
☛ Have adequate table space for everyone to have room to work.
☛ Have adequate craft supplies (including extras for "mistakes").
☛ Duplicate sample project instructions (perhaps with diagrams, depending on the difficulty of the project) so that each guest can have a copy for reference.
☛ Prepare food and beverages ahead of time so that you can enjoy the party, too!

For craft project ideas and directions, refer to any of the following books: *Book of Christmas Decorations, Christmas Is Coming,* volumes I - III, *Christmas Ornaments, Decorating Craft Ideas for Christmas 1984, Penny Whistle Christmas Party Book,* and *Spirit of Christmas: Creative Holiday Ideas,* volumes I - III. (See Resources for details.)

Keep refreshments simple. Coffee and tea or punch with Christmas cookies, iced brownies, or a delicious cake is enough!

Christmas Craft and Dessert Party is a great way to get together with women friends!
Debbie Hall, formerly of Memphis, Tennessee, originated this party idea.

Chapter 33

Great Cookie Swap

This party is a great way to supply your own and all your friends' cookie needs for a whole holiday season. Trade batches of Christmas cookies while getting together for a fun evening of eating and socializing.

Meet at a favorite restaurant for dinner—as a reward for finishing Christmas baking! Then, everyone returns to your home for a cookie exchange. Each woman brings one variety of her favorite Christmas cookie with one dozen each individually wrapped on separate paper plates. You and your guests swap until everyone has traded away all of her own cookies for dozens of different kinds of homemade cookies!

Invitation Ideas

Use pretty preprinted invitations for this gathering. Try to find invitations with cookies or other baked goods on the front. If you prefer, make up and duplicate a flyer cut from card stock or construction paper in the shape of a Christmas cookie.

Include your name and address, as well as the name and address of the restaurant, the date and time of the party, and a telephone number for an R.S.V.P. You'll also want to specify exactly how many dozen cookies each guest should bring and how they should be packaged. The atmosphere of the restaurant you choose will determine whether the gathering is casual or more dressy.

Setting the Mood

Decorations: For this celebration, go wild with cookies! Hang cookies, decorated and plain, all over your Christmas tree. (Make holes at the top of cookies before baking, string colorful ribbons through, and tie to the tree with bows.) Or, use permanent decorations that look like cookies. Add other edibles—or faux edibles—such as strings of popcorn and cranberries, candy canes, and gilded nuts. Decorate an indoor wreath similarly, and adorn a wreath of greenery for the front door with sturdy cookies sprayed with a clear sealant. Decorate a mantel with gingerbread men marching through greenery, and hang rows of cookies strung on a colorful ribbon across kitchen and party windows. A Christmas tablecloth and a Christmas cookie jar "spilling over" with a variety of cookies makes an easy centerpiece, or use a collection of cookie jars for a clever decoration.

Music: Christmas songs and carols played softly in the background are perfect at this gathering.

Enhancements: Ask each guest to pack a duplicated copy of her cookie recipe with each dozen. And, since everyone's baking anyway, ask each guest to bring an additional dozen cookies to add to a "sampling table" for women to taste-test!

Special Activities

The emphasis of this celebration is sharing—not only a meal, but also dozens of home-made cookies. The women meet at the restaurant for a leisurely meal, and reconvene at the hostess's home for the cookie exchange. If guests don't already know each other, use simple name tags cut in the shape of a cookie.

The simplest method for conducting the cookie swap? Have each guest make a plate-for-plate cookie trade with every other woman until everyone has traded off all of her cookies. Guests will take home cookies on the paper plates inside the same box or container in which they brought their own cookies.

Theme Variations

Instead of simply trading cookies, allow winners of simple games such as Bingo to choose a plate of cookies each time they win a round. This takes longer than simple trade-offs, but can add even more fun to the evening.

Limitations and Logistics

The limitation on this party is space—the exchange works best if each participant has some area, perhaps a card table, on which she can place the cookies she brought as well as the plates of cookies she receives. In addition to tables, kitchen countertops, coffee tables, dining room and kitchen tables, and flat surfaces in adjoining rooms can also be used. The only other restriction on this celebration may be financial—for friends who may not be able to afford a restaurant dinner. In such a case, switch the meal to your home and have everyone contribute to a planned potluck dinner.

Six to ten women is an excellent size for this party. Your only preparation is making luncheon or dinner reservations, decorating, baking and wrapping your own cookies for sharing, and making sure there is an area for each guest to distribute and receive cookies.

Because guests have already shared a restaurant meal, refreshments can be kept at a minimum: cookie samples with hot or cold beverages—perhaps frosty cold mugs of milk or hot coffee or tea. Use festive paper goods for easy cleanup.

Great Cookie Swap is a "women only" activity!

Chapter 34

Baskets of Joy

If you want to experience the true spirit of giving, send out invitations asking guests to gather sample-size beauty supplies and toiletries. On the day of the party, everyone will bring what they have collected, along with an attractive basket. As the afternoon gets under way, each woman fills her basket with a selection of items, decorates the filled basket, and attaches a handwritten note with good wishes for a happy holiday season. As a finale, deliver the baskets to elderly women and shut-ins whom the hostesses have previously decided to give them to. No one spends much time or money and the party doesn't last more than an hour and a half. But every Basket of Joy fulfills the purpose of its name!

Invitations

A pretty flyer, duplicated on paper with Christmas decorations, is ideal for this gathering. In addition to the who, when, and where, be specific about the what and why!

Ask guests to bring along a pretty basket and explain in detail exactly what type and how many toiletries or other items they should collect and bring. Add a word about attire—casual but festive with a Christmas motif to cheer up basket recipients—plus an R.S.V.P. and telephone number so you'll be sure to have enough craft supplies on hand. Send out invitations at least six weeks in advance (eight is even better) so that guests have plenty of time to collect items to fill baskets.

Setting the Mood

Decorations: Use baskets as the decorative motif for this celebration. Decorate your Christmas tree with tiny baskets, red and green bows and lights, and rattan ornaments. Place large baskets, some filled with potpourri (and simmer more potpourri on the stove), others with pine cones on countertops and coffee tables. Put similar baskets on the mantel and the hearth. Light a cozy fire if you have a fireplace. Finally, fill a half-basket (flat on one side) with natural, nonbreakable ornaments, and fasten it securely to the front door to welcome guests to your party.

Music: To add to the joyful spirit of the afternoon, encourage guests to sing Christmas carols as they fill and wrap baskets. If they don't wish to sing, play recorded Christmas music in the background.

Enhancements: Send a remembrance home with each guest. One idea: Place small poinsettia plants inside basket holders (decorated if you wish) and give these to guests as they depart.

A thoughtful gesture for retailers who donated samples and supplies: Have women write down the names and addresses of establishments where they received these items. After the party, drop them a brief note of thanks for their kindness and generosity.

Special Activities

Ask guests to contact retail establishments for donations of product samples for a specified number of baskets—as many guests as you've invited. (Beauty salons, drug, grocery, department, and discount stores often have sample or trial size toiletries and other items applicable for these baskets. When they understand the nature of such a project, they will often go out of their way to provide items.) Guests may also choose to purchase trial or sample sizes themselves. In addition, each guest should purchase an inexpensive medium-sized basket with a handle.

As the women arrive at your home, have each put her supplies together in categories on one table: shampoo samples together, purse-size tissue packs, tea bags, and so on. At the first spot on this table, place decorative shredded tissue paper to cushion the toiletries. In assembly line fashion, each guest goes through the line, all the way around the table, placing one of each item in her tissue-lined basket until it's complete.

Down the center of another table or two, you'll have everything ready to decorate baskets: cellophane wrap, ribbon, cards, envelopes, colored pens, and scissors. Everyone can gather around to wrap and finish baskets, write out cards, seal them in envelopes, and attach the notes to baskets. (Punch holes in envelope corners, run the tip of the ribbon through the hole, and tie this into a bow on the basket.)

After basket assembly is completed, invite guests to help themselves to light refreshments. Everybody then piles into designated cars and vans to deliver Baskets of Joy to the elderly and shut-ins for whom they're designated. This can be done most efficiently by preplanning routes according to the proximity of the recipients.

Limitations and Logistics

An even dozen is an ideal number of guests to hold this gathering in a home, but more or less will work equally well. If this party project is carried out on a much larger scale—for twenty-five or more participants—you may want to set up long tables in a church or business meeting area so there is plenty of room for the basket-assembly process.

Beforehand, stock up on small note cards with envelopes and craft supplies to decorate baskets: decorative, colorful, regular or shredded tissue paper, rolls of colored cellophane wrap, and contrasting ribbon in sufficient quantities to complete a basket for each participant. You also may wish to purchase flavored teas and hard candies, or other similar sealed food items to add to baskets.

Refreshments should be as simple as possible to allow you to devote the majority of your time to the basket project. Set up a small buffet table covered with a Christmas tablecloth. Use festive paper plates, napkins, and cups. Serve a hot or cold beverage and a small snack—from a pretty basket—such as cranberry, zucchini nut, or pumpkin bread with cream cheese.

Baskets of Joy is an ideal reach-out project for a group of women friends.

Chapter 35

Open House for Seniors

enior citizens often can be a somewhat neglected group. If you love your senior citizen friends and Christmas, put on a special midafternoon Open House for Seniors. The spotlight is on them. The whole idea of the celebration is to help make them feel valued, special, and loved! Arrange transportation to and from the Senior Center, prepare a buffet of finger foods, arrange for entertainment, and treat your special guests as if they were royalty. At the end of the party give each one a huge hug and tuck a special remembrance into the hands of each guest. Both you and they will experience the true joy of Christmas!

Invitation Ideas

Choose a preprinted Open House invitation, or make up an attractive flyer and duplicate it. Either way, be sure the words are large and clear enough to be easily read. Include all pertinent information: your name and address, and the date and time (both beginning and end) of your gathering. Add an R.S.V.P. with your telephone number. Put in a note about attire: Encourage your senior guests to dress comfortably and warmly—especially since they will be outside briefly when they arrive and leave. And because some seniors love to get all dressed up for an occasion, let them know that this is fine, too.

Setting the Mood

Decorations: Adorn your home with traditional Christmas decorations of red, white, and green. Put up a beautiful tree with old-fashioned ornaments, and string popcorn and cranberries on it. If you have a fireplace, build a roaring fire. Use old-fashioned and handmade ornaments nestled in greenery on the mantel and staircase, and place manger scenes around the room. Put your prettiest Christmas wreath on the front door and attach a handmade sign: "Welcome, Seniors!"

Music: The entertainers will provide the main music for this party in a way that the seniors will love. But also offer guests the opportunity to join in singing Christmas carols at some other point during the afternoon. Ask a skilled pianist to accompany them. Song sheets are optional; most seniors know the words to far more verses than we do! During the rest of your Open House, play traditional recorded Christmas songs as just the right background music to top off a wonderful afternoon!

Enhancements: Send each guest home with a remembrance of the Open House. Loaves of bread or other baked goods wrapped festively are a perfect choice.

Special Activities

As your guests arrive, greet them warmly—at the door or even at curbside. Ask a few mature high schoolers or junior high students to help you with the party. They can take their coats and hats and place them in an adjoining room. Have your Santa's elves help each guest find a comfortable seat for the afternoon. After everyone has arrived, invite guests to help themselves to the buffet or have Santa's elves deliver a beautifully filled plate to each, depending on each individual guest's mobility. As the seniors enjoy their refreshments, the entertainment can begin.

Make arrangements with a local school glee club or junior choir to perform. After the group sings, offer refills to guests and invite the performers to have some refreshments and mingle with the seniors. At the appointed time, thank all of the guests for coming, signaling the end of the party. At this point, your elves can assist guests with their coats and other cold-weather gear and escort them back to curbside.

Limitations and Logistics

Any number that will fit comfortably into your entertaining area is fine, perhaps twelve to twenty seniors, space permitting. You might invite a specific segment of people within a larger organization so that everyone in that group will receive an invitation.

Only three minor limitations must be considered. If weather conditions on the day of the Open House are icy and bitter cold, it probably is better to reschedule for a day when the ice has thawed. (It would be tragic to have guests slip and hurt themselves on the ice!) Also, you must provide a chair for every guest. This is mandatory. And you must have enough helpers to come to the aid of less mobile guests.

You'll need to complete a number of tasks before the day of the Open House:

☛ Secure reliable and safe transportation for the seniors to and from your house. (City government organizations or the seniors' facility may provide this service.)

☛ Make provisions for some sort of entertainment that will especially appeal to seniors—an ensemble of young people from a local school or another organization. (Some groups of this nature charge to perform, others do not; just be sure to ask and get all the details.)

☞ Make adequate space in your entertaining area for the performance.

☞ Make sure there is a chair for every senior.

☞ Prepare a simple buffet of finger foods only.

Balancing a plateful of elaborate food, silverware, and a beverage may prove too challenging for guests; strictly finger foods are imperative at this gathering. Make the decision ahead of time whether guests will serve themselves from the buffet, or helpers will serve them a plate already filled with goodies from the kitchen.

If you have a buffet, cover the table with a bright cloth and place a small Christmas tree decorated with old-fashioned ornaments on it as a centerpiece. Serve food on sturdy festive paper goods, and be sure to provide enough small tables near the guests to hold their beverages and plates.

A simple menu for this gathering might be tea sandwiches, crackers or chips and dip, pumpkin and cranberry breads, Christmas cookies, punch or coffee and tea.

Open House for Seniors can be held by a group of women, couples, or singles as a reach-out project.
Patti Beckman, of Irvine, California, originated the Open House for Seniors.

Chapter 36

Cajun Christmas Feast

If you've ever visited New Orleans, "the City that Care Forgot," you know there's nothing like Cajun hospitality. A Cajun Christmas Feast is an opportunity to entertain guests with the legendary food and exceptional warmth of Louisiana. To carry out this idea, encourage guests to throw away their cares for the evening and celebrate Christmas New Orleans style!

Serve a fabulous New Orleans-style dinner, complete with pralines. Then, read guests *Cajun Night Before Christmas*—hilarious!—and have a Cajun gift exchange. As the evening comes to a close, send friends home with favors—a Cajun coloring book for guests' children is ideal. Even if your guests have never been to New Orleans before, they'll get a taste of the city with your Cajun Christmas Feast.

Invitation Ideas

If you live in the South, pick large fresh green leaves from your magnolia trees and preserve the leaves with glycerin. If you live anywhere else in the country, purchase artificial magnolia bushes at a craft store and use the largest leaves to write on as invitations. Enclose a tiny bit of Spanish moss with each invitation and use an oversized envelope.

Use a gold paint pen to write at the top, "*Joie de Vivre* " (joy of living), and on the next line, "Because you enjoy life, we request your company at a Cajun Christmas Feast." This party requires an R.S.V.P., so add that with your telephone number. Tell guests what to wear (choose among everyday casual, fancy, the old South, or a Mardi Gras costume) and request that they bring a small wrapped present that is somehow related to New Orleans or the Cajun theme for a gift exchange.

If you use real magnolia leaves, take special care in mailing invitations. Or better yet, if time permits, deliver the invitations in person.

Setting the Mood

Decorations: Decorate your entertaining area with Christmas magnolias, real or good artificial ones. Drape Spanish moss (available at craft stores) through Christmas garlands around the house and adorn your Christmas tree with ornaments characteristic of Louisiana—miniature dolls, alligators, crawfish, and so on. Dress the serving table with a centerpiece of massed magnolia plants with Spanish moss around their bases. Use a pretty linen tablecloth and your finest china and crystal. Use one or more beautiful Christmas magnolias at guests' tables for centerpieces, with Spanish moss around the base of the pots.

Music: Cajun music is called Zydeco, a unique blend of blues, jazz, and folk rock. Check your local music store for cassettes or compact discs with Christmas Cajun music or try to find *Cajun Dance Favorites, Best of Jazz Fest,* and *The Best of Cajun Country.* If they're unavailable in your area, contact Werlein's Music Store in New Orleans (telephone 504-883-5080).

Enhancements: Lagniappe, a small gift that is traditionally the Cajun shopkeeper's gesture of goodwill, is a must for guests as they leave. It can be very inexpensive: a wrapped praline, a packet of Cajun spices, or the *Cajun Night Before Christmas* coloring book.

Special Activities

As guests arrive, greet them with southern hospitality. If you wish, provide magnolia leaf name tags with names written in gold paint pen on them. Offer guests a cup of punch, and encourage them to mingle until dinner is served.

Enjoying the Cajun feast and experiencing true southern hospitality are the primary focuses of the evening. Make it fun! As dinner winds down and dessert is served, read *Cajun Night Before Christmas,* in the condensed version (see order information at the end of this chapter)—in your best New Orleans accent, of course!

After dinner, guests can move back to the entertaining area and start the Cajun Gift Exchange—a modified version of the white elephant exchange (see the White Elephant Party chapter). Start the exchange with one guest choosing a wrapped gift from under the Christmas tree. She unwraps it and decides whether or not she wants to keep it. If not, she gives it to the person on her left and chooses and unwraps another present until she finds one she likes. The second woman (to the left of the first) can keep the unwrapped gift she was given or pass it on and make another choice from under the tree, and so on. The exchange is over when every guest has a gift she likes.

Limitations and Logistics

Any number that can be seated comfortably in your dining or entertaining area is just right. Especially for a large crowd, finances might be a restriction on this celebration if you're having the meal catered or ordering food mixes from Louisiana. With a little courage and a Cajun cookbook, however, you should be able tackle the New Orleans-style menu yourself (or with the help of a friend) and cut down the cost significantly.

Some preparation hints:

•   Unless you are a native of Louisiana and know how to "cook Cajun," you'll probably need to do mail-order preparation. (See the mail-order vendor information at the end of this chapter; their wonderful products will convince your guests you "cook Cajun." If you choose to prepare all the dishes from scratch, check your local library for one or more of the excellent Cajun cookbooks listed at the end of this chapter—or you might want to invest in several.)

•   If you plan to read *Cajun Night Before Christmas,* call or write (see chapter's end) for the book, coloring book, or audio cassette.

•   Search out lagniappe— you'll want them to have a Cajun flavor. Look for Cajun spices, a simple Cajun cookbook, New Orleans French bread or gumbo mix, canapé cutters for New Orleans-style pastries, and so on. Many of these items are available from specialty or gourmet cooking shops.

Your buffet of delicious Cajun dishes should be a real feast—served with a generous helping of southern hospitality. It might include some or all of the following dishes: Orleanian soup, French Quarter salad with artichoke dressing, gumbo with filé, etouffé, crawfish pie, and jambalaya, followed by pralines with coffee and tea.

Cajun Christmas Feast is a fun celebration for couples, singles, and women only. Beverly Brandon, a native of New Orleans, introduced me to a Cajun Christmas Feast.

Cajun Sources

FOOD

Aunt Sally's

810 Decatur Street
New Orleans, Louisiana 70116
504-524-3373
This gift store in the French Quarter in New Orleans operates a mail-order business shipping pralines, beignet mix, souvenirs of New Orleans, and Vieux Carré gift items. You can find the perfect dessert here. Call or write to request their free mail-order catalog.

K-Paul's—Chef Paul Prudhomme's Louisiana Mail Order

824 Distributors Row
New Orleans, Louisiana 70183-0342
800-457-2857
Call to request the free eighteen-page mail-order catalog of Prudhomme's Cajun foods and seasonings.

Louisiana Fish Fry Products, Ltd.

5267 Plank Road
Baton Rouge, Louisiana 70805
504-356-2905
Call or write to request their mail-order brochure of approximately twenty items ($5 minimum order) from gumbo to etouffé.

Luzianne Blue Plate Foods

640 Magazine
New Orleans, Louisiana 70130
504-524-6131
Call or write for menu ideas and information about Luzianne products. The company has produced Louisiana food and beverage products since 1903.

Mam Papaul's

Louisiana Gourmet Enterprises, Inc.
P.O. Box 97
Hahnville, Louisiana 70057
800-EAT-KJUN or 504-783-2446
Call to request their free mail-order catalog. You must purchase a minimum of twelve packages of various foods.

Miss Mary's Pralines 'n' Things
P.O. Box 53792
Lafayette, Louisiana 70505
318-234-2715
Call or write to order any of Miss Mary's gourmet desserts, special granola, and more.

COOKBOOKS

....

The Evolution of Cajun and Creole Cuisine
(Baton Rouge, Louisiana, John D. Folse, 1990). $22.95 including shipping and handling. Make check payable to and order ISBN 0-96251-5205 from:
Friends of LPB
P.O. Box 3122
Baton Rouge, Louisiana 70821

From A Louisiana Kitchen by Holly Berkowitz Clegg (Dallas, Wimmer Brothers, 1991).
$9.95 plus $3.00 shipping and handling. Make check payable to and order from:
Maison Blanche
P.O. Drawer 91013
Baton Rouge, Louisiana 70821

Jambalaya
(New Orleans, The Junior League of New Orleans, 1983). $11.95 plus $2.00 shipping and handling ($2.50 S. & H. for gift wrap). Make check payable to and order from:
The Junior League of New Orleans
4319 Carondelet Street
New Orleans, Louisiana 70115

GREAT READING
FOR A CAJUN CHRISTMAS FEAST:

....

Cajun Night Before Christmas
Coloring book (with abbreviated story) $2.75; hardback book, $12.95; audio cassette, $9.95. Available at some bookstores across the country, these can be ordered directly from the publisher. Call Pelican Publishing Company (for book orders only): 800-843-1724

Appendix

Recipes for Parties

Snacks and Hors d'Oeuvres

Holiday Smokies

1 package Little Smokies sausages
1 lb. bacon
1/2 box brown sugar
Toothpicks

Cut bacon strips into thirds; widthwise. Wrap one piece of bacon around each Little Smokie and secure with a toothpick. Place in a 13 x 9 x 2" baking pan. Sprinkle approximately 1/2 box of brown sugar evenly over Smokies. Bake at 350° for 30 – 45 minutes.

Salmon Ball

1 can (14 3/4 oz.) salmon
1 package (8 oz.) cream cheese, softened
1 Tbsp. lemon juice
2 tsp. finely grated onion
1 tsp. horseradish
1/4 tsp. salt
1/4 tsp. liquid smoke
1/2 - 1 C. chopped pecans
3 Tbsp. finely chopped parsley

Drain and flake salmon, removing skin and bones. Combine salmon, cream cheese, lemon juice, onion, horseradish, salt, and liquid smoke. Mix thoroughly with a mixer or by hand. Chill for several hours. Combine chopped pecans and cut parsley and sprinkle on waxed paper. Shape the salmon mixture into two small balls and roll in the nut mixture. Chill well. Serve with assorted crackers. (Especially good with Vegetable Thins.)

Shrimp Dip

1 can (4 1/4 oz.) small broken shrimp
1 package Good Seasons Italian Dressing Mix
1 package (8 oz.) cream cheese
1 carton (8 oz.) sour cream
2 Tbsp. lemon juice

Allow cream cheese to reach room temperature. Blend all ingredients on low speed with an electric mixer. Chill overnight or for several hours. Serve with fresh vegetables, crackers, or corn chips. Makes about 2 cups.

Spinach Dip in Sourdough Round

1 box (10 oz.) frozen spinach
1/2 bunch green onions, chopped
2 cups real mayonnaise
1 tsp. garlic powder
1/2 tsp. lemon juice
1/2 tsp. Worcestershire sauce
1– 1 1/2 tsp. seasoned salt
2 round loaves sourdough bread

Defrost spinach. Drain well and squeeze spinach in a clean dish towel or cheesecloth to remove all remaining water. Tear into small pieces, removing large stems. Mix spinach with remaining ingredients except bread. Chill mixture for several hours or overnight. Cut one sourdough loaf into chunks. Hollow out the other loaf and mound in dip. Serve with loaf chunks and crisp raw vegetables such as zucchini, carrots, celery, cucumber slices, cauliflower, and broccoli. (If preferred, this dip can be served in a hollowed-out head of red cabbage.) Serves 12 – 15 or more.

Guacamole Dip

2 large ripe avocados
2 Tbsp. finely chopped onion
1/2 tsp. minced garlic
1/2 tsp. Tabasco sauce
1/2 tsp. salt
2 Tbsp. lemon juice
1 Tbsp. mayonnaise or sour cream
1/2 cup finely chopped celery, optional

Combine all ingredients. Blend until smooth with a mixer or in a blender. Chill thoroughly. Serve with corn chips, etc. Makes about 1 1/2 cups.

Party Cheese Balls

1 package (8 oz.) cream cheese, softened
1 pound Velveeta cheese
1- 2 cups pecans, chopped
2 cloves garlic
1 Tbsp. pimiento, finely chopped, optional
1 Tbsp. green pepper, finely chopped, optional
Chili powder

Soften and beat cream cheese. Add all other ingredients except chili powder. Mix by hand. Chill thoroughly. Divide the mixture into two equal parts; roll each into a ball or a log. Sprinkle chili powder over a piece of waxed paper, and roll each ball or log to coat lightly and evenly. Chill until firm. Especially good served on Ritz crackers. Makes 2 large balls or logs.

Crab Dip

1 can (6 oz.) crab or artificial crabmeat
1 carton (8 oz.) sour cream
2 tsp. horseradish
2 Tbsp. bottled Italian dressing
1/2 tsp. pepper

Drain crabmeat well. Mix all ingredients together using a mixer or blender. Chill thoroughly. Serve with fresh vegetables, crackers, or chips. Makes about 2 cups.

Smokey Egg Dip

3/4 cup real mayonnaise
1 tsp. liquid smoke
2 drops Tabasco
1 Tbsp. vinegar
1 Tbsp. prepared mustard

2 Tbsp. Worcestershire sauce
2 Tbsp. margarine or butter
1 tsp. salt
1/4 tsp. pepper
12 hard-cooked eggs
1/4 tsp. cayenne pepper

Place all ingredients except eggs and cayenne in blender container. Cut eggs into several pieces; add eggs slowly while blender is running on low speed. Continue blending until smooth. Chill. Sprinkle cayenne over dip before serving. Serve with fresh vegetables, crackers, etc. Makes about 3 cups.

Entrees

Barbequed Brisket
1 large beef brisket
Liquid smoke
Onion salt
Garlic salt
Worcestershire sauce
Barbeque sauce

Two nights before serving, wipe brisket with a damp cloth, brush with liquid smoke, and place in a large glass baking pan. Sprinkle with onion salt and garlic salt. Cover with plastic wrap and let stand in refrigerator overnight. The next morning sprinkle with Worcestershire sauce, and cover tightly with foil. Bake at 275°, cooking 35-45 minutes per pound. Cool; refrigerate overnight. The next day skim off all fat, slice the meat while cold, preferably with an electric knife, and place back in baking pan with meat juice. Pour barbeque sauce over

meat, cover, and heat thoroughly. Serve hot or cold as a main dish or in sandwiches. Serves 6 - 8 or more.

Easy Lasagna
1– 2 pounds lean ground beef (or ground turkey)
1 jar (32 oz.) spaghetti sauce
8 ounces lasagna noodles, uncooked
1 carton (16 oz.) cottage cheese
1 carton (8 oz.) plain yogurt
1 package (8 oz.) Mozzarella cheese, grated
1/2 cup grated Parmesan cheese
1 cup water

Preheat oven to 350°. Brown ground beef and drain off all excess fat. Spread 1 cup spaghetti sauce in a greased 13 x 9 x 2" baking pan. Blend together in a small bowl the cottage cheese and the plain yogurt. Layer one-third each of uncooked noodles, cottage cheese-yogurt mixture, ground beef, Mozzarella, remaining spaghetti sauce and Parmesan. Repeat these layers twice more. Pour water around the sides of the baking pan. Cover tightly with foil and bake at 350° for 1 hour. Remove foil and bake 15 minutes longer or until noodles are tender. Let stand 10 - 20 minutes before serving. Makes 12 or more generous servings. Note: You can also add diced cooked chicken or turkey to the recipe to add more protein and flavor. This lasagna freezes beautifully. Bake for 40 minutes, cool, and freeze. Remove from freezer, defrost, and bake for about 30 minutes covered. Take foil off and bake about 10 minutes longer. Then let stand just 10 minutes before serving.

Cheese Fondue

1 (10 3/4 oz.) can cheddar cheese soup, undiluted
1/2 - 1 cup commercial French onion dip
1- 1 1/2 cups grated sharp cheddar cheese (4 oz. or
*   more)*
1/2 tsp. dry mustard
1/8 tsp. cayenne pepper
1 large loaf fresh French bread cut in 1-inch cubes

Combine all ingredients except French bread in a saucepan or in the fondue pot, and blend thoroughly. Do not add salt, as onion dip makes it salty enough. Mixture will get hot more quickly in the saucepan on stove. Place over low heat, stirring constantly, until cheese melts and mixture is hot. Transfer from pan to fondue pot. Keep heat very low, checking to see that it is hot but not burning on the bottom. Spear a bread cube with fondue fork, twirl in cheese mixture, drain, cool, and eat. Makes 4 or more servings.

Beef Fondue

3 pounds boneless beef sirloin or tenderloin or 1/2
*   pound of meat per adult serving*
Cooking oil (corn, cottonseed, or peanut oil) or half
*   butter and half cooking oil*

Trim fat from meat; cut into bite-sized cubes. Refrigerate until 20 minutes before cooking time. Fill fondue pot about 1/2 full with oil or butter-and-oil mixture. Heat oil on stove to 360°. If butter-oil mixture is used, heat slowly until butter bubbles and mixture turns a golden color. Set fondue pot on stand over moderately high direct heat, and maintain heat. Spear a cube of beef with fondue fork; hold it in the hot oil until cooked to the desired doneness, 1 to 3 minutes. Remove meat from fork and cool slightly. Serve with favorite barbeque or other sauce. Serves about 6.

Roast Turkey

To prepare the fresh or thawed turkey, remove the neck and giblets from the cavity of the bird. Place the giblets, except the liver, in a saucepan with seasoning and cover with water. Let simmer 2 hours, adding the liver the last 30 minutes. Save the broth for gravy and dressing. Chop giblets to add to gravy.

Rinse the turkey. Rub inside with 1/4 tsp. salt per pound. Instead of stuffing, place a few slices of onion, a stalk of celery, and a sprig of parsley in the cavity. Fasten neck skin to back of turkey; tuck legs under band of skin at tail. Bend wing tips under body or fasten to body. Place bird on rack in roasting pan. Brush entire bird with melted butter. Cover top and side of bird with a loose foil tent. Place in 325° oven, and bake as follows:

Ready-to-cook Weight	Total Cooking Time*	Number of Servings
6 to 8 pounds	3 to 3 1/2 hours	6 to 10
8 to 12 pounds	4 to 4 1/2 hours	11 to 20
12 to 16 pounds	5 to 5 1/2 hours	21 to 30
16 to 20 pounds	6 to 6 1/2 hours	31 to 40
20 to 24 pounds	6 1/2 to 7 hours	More than 40

*These times are approximate for roasting fresh thawed birds. Roast until tender.

Test for doneness about 30 minutes before timetable indicates. When turkey is done, thickest part of the drumstick feels soft when drumstick is twisted. Turkey is done when thermometer registers 185°.

Seafood Cassserole

1/4 cup butter or margarine
1 cup chopped celery
1/4 cup chopped onion
1 small green pepper, chopped
3 Tbsp. butter or margarine
3 Tbsp. flour
1 1/2 cups milk
1 tsp. Worcestershire sauce
3/4 tsp. salt
Dash cayenne or Tobasco
1 cup mayonnaise
1 can (4 1/4 oz.)tiny shrimp
1 can (6 oz.) crabmeat
1 can (12 1/4 oz. or 9 1/4 oz.) white meat tuna
2 cups cooked white rice
Buttered bread crumbs

Sauté celery, onion, and green pepper slowly in 1/4 cup butter or margarine for about 10 minutes. Melt 3 Tbsp. butter or margarine in saucepan over low heat. Blend in flour. Add milk all at once. Cook quickly, stirring constantly, until mixture thickens and bubbles. Add Worcestershire, salt, and cayenne or Tobasco, and blend. Stir the mayonnaise into this mixture. Add shrimp, crabmeat, and tuna. Add the rice, and blend together thoroughly. Place in greased casserole dish, sprinkle in buttered crumbs on top, and bake at 300° for 45 - 50 minutes. Serves 6 to 8.

French Onion Soup

6 medium onions
Butter or margarine
Salt and pepper
3 (10 3/4 oz. each) cans bouillon
French bread croutons
4 slices Monterey Jack cheese
Parmesan cheese

Slice onions in rings; sauté with butter in a large kettle or Dutch oven over low heat for about 10-15 minutes or until lightly browned. Stir to cook evenly. Add bouillon, and simmer for 15 - 30 minutes or longer. Season with pepper. Pour into "bake and serve bowls." Float French bread croutons on top. Cover top of each bowl with a slice of Monterey Jack cheese, and sprinkle generously with Parmesan. Bake at 375° for about 5 minutes, or until the cheese melts. Serves 4.

Chicken (or Turkey) Corn Chowder

1/4 cup butter or margarine
4 medium onions, sliced
5 medium potatoes (with or without skin), cut in small pieces
2 stalks celery, finely sliced or chopped
1 Tbsp. salt
1/2 tsp. pepper
2 cups water
1 chicken bouillon cube
5 cups whole milk
2 cans (16 1/2 oz. each) whole-kernel corn
1 can (16 1/2 oz.) cream-style corn
1/4 tsp. thyme
1 cup light cream or half-and-half
1 1/2 tsp. paprika
3 cups cut-up cooked chicken or turkey
Parsley

In a large saucepan or kettle, melt butter or margarine and sauté onions until golden, stirring often. Add potatoes, celery, salt, pepper, water, and bouillon cube. Cook covered for 15 minutes or until vegetables are tender. Add milk, both kinds of corn, thyme, cream, paprika, and chicken or turkey. Heat thoroughly just until bubbly. Serve with parsley snipped over top. Serves 8 to 10.

Quick Chili

1 pound lean ground beef
1 Tbsp. dried minced onion
1 Tbsp. dried minced green pepper, optional
1/2 cup old-fashioned rolled oats
2 cans (16 oz. each) tomatoes
2 cans (15 oz. each) pinto beans
1 - 1 1/2 tsp. salt
2 Tbsp. chili powder

Brown ground beef in a large skillet, breaking it into small chunks. Drain off all excess grease. Add remaining ingredients, and mix well. Cover and simmer for 30 minutes, stirring occasionally. Serves 6 to 8.

Cheese-Egg Custard

4 to 6 eggs, beaten
1 1/2 - 2 cups whole milk
Scant 1/2 tsp. salt
1 - 2 cups grated sharp cheddar cheese
1/4 tsp. dry mustard
1/8 tsp. pepper

Mix all ingredients. Bake in a greased 6 x 10" glass baking dish at 325° for 35 - 40 minutes, or until almost firm. The top will be light golden brown. Holds well. Serves 6 or more.

Quiche Lorraine

1 deep-dish pie crust or miniature pie crust shells, unbaked
6 - 8 slices cooked lean bacon or diced ham
1 - 2 cups grated cheese, cheddar or Mozzarella
1/2 onion, finely chopped, or equivalent in dry onion flakes
1 1/2 cups whole milk or half-and-half
5 eggs
Salt and pepper, to taste

In the deep-dish or mini pie crust shells, sprinkle diced bacon or ham, cheese, and onion. In a blender or mixer blend milk, eggs, and salt and pepper for 1 minute. Pour over other ingredients in crust. Bake at 350° for 45 minutes or until just barely firm. Made in the large pie shell, this recipe serves 6 or more.

Salads

Frosted Berry Mold

2 cups boiling water
1 package (6 oz.) cherry or raspberry Jell-O
1 package (10 oz.) frozen strawberries, with juice
1 can (16 oz.) whole cranberry sauce
1 cup chopped pecans
1/2 cup real mayonnaise
1/2 cup sour cream

Combine water with Jell-O, stirring until Jell-O is dissolved. Add strawberries with their juice, cranberry sauce, and pecans. Place in a 6 x 10" glass dish and chill until set. Blend mayonnaise and sour cream together thoroughly, and spread over top. Refrigerate until ready to serve. Serves 8.

Hearty Spinach Salad

1 large package fresh spinach
1 can (14 oz.) bean sprouts, drained
1 can (8 oz.) sliced water chestnuts
1 pound lean bacon, cooked crisp and crumbled
2 hard-boiled eggs, sliced or diced
1 purple onion, in thinly sliced rings, optional

If necessary, rewash spinach and drain thoroughly. Destem and tear it into bite-sized pieces. Toss together spinach pieces, bean sprouts, and water chestnuts. After dressing is poured over and salad is tossed, arrange egg slices, crumbled bacon, and onion rings on top.

Dressing for Spinach Salad

3/4 cup sugar
1/4 cup vinegar, flavored if desired
1 cup salad oil
1 small onion, grated
2 tsp. Worcestershire sauce
1/3 cup ketchup

Shake, whip, or blend all ingredients together thoroughly. This blends well if refrigerated overnight. Recipe makes more than enough dressing for the salad, so use according to taste.

Layered Strawberry Banana Jell-O Salad

1 package (6 oz.) strawberry Jell-O
1 cup boiling water
2 packages (16 oz. each) frozen strawberries, with juice
1 can (20 oz.) crushed pineapple, drained
3 ripe bananas, mashed
1 cup chopped nuts, optional
1 carton (16 oz.) sour cream

Dissolve strawberry Jell-O in boiling water. When completely dissolved, add strawberries with their juice, drained crushed pineapple, mashed bananas, and the chopped nuts, if desired. Blend thoroughly. Pour approximately 1/3 to 1/2 of the Jell-O mixture into the bottom of a glass 13 x 9 x 2" dish. Place in refrigerator until firm. Spread the carton of sour cream (thinned with a little milk, if necessary) evenly over Jell-O. Pour remaining Jell-O carefully over the sour cream, covering it completely. Refrigerate again until firm. Makes 18 to 24 servings. Note: This recipe can be cut in half, if desired, and prepared in an 8 x 8" or 9 x 9" pan.

Twenty-Four Hour Fruit Salad

3 egg yolks
2 Tbsp. sugar
2 Tbsp. vinegar
2 Tbsp. pineapple juice
1 Tbsp. butter or margarine
1/4 tsp. salt
2 1/2 cups miniature marshmallows
1 jar (17 oz.) pitted white cherries, drained
1 can (20 oz.) crushed pineapple, drained

1 can (11 oz.) mandarin orange sections, drained
1 cup whipping cream, whipped

Beat egg yolks; add sugar, vinegar, pineapple juice, butter, and salt. Cook on medium heat until thick, stirring constantly. Cool. Fold in marshmallows, fruit, and whipped cream. Chill 24 hours before serving. Makes 12 servings.

Three Bean Salad

1 or 2 cans (16 oz. each) cut green beans
1 can wax beans
1 can kidney beans
1 red Bermuda onion, sliced thin or chopped
1/4 cup diced pimiento and/or green pepper, optional
1/2 cup sugar
1/2 cup salad oil
2/3 cup vinegar
1/2 tsp. Worcestershire sauce
1 tsp. salt
1/4 tsp. pepper

Drain all beans and place them in a large bowl or refrigerator container with the other vegetables. Mix remaining ingredients thoroughly, and pour over beans. Cover tightly and allow to marinate overnight or longer. Stir from time to time. Serve thoroughly chilled. Serves 10 - 12.

Parsley Vegetable Wreath

1 small Styrofoam ring, such as one used for a wreath
Toothpicks
2 - 3 bunches of fresh parsley, washed

Fresh vegetables such as small carrot strips, cauliflower and broccoli flowerets, radishes, zucchini slices, cherry tomatoes, green pepper slices, etc., washed and cut

Place Styrofoam ring in the center of a nice serving platter. Use toothpicks to secure sprigs of parsley to the Styrofoam ring, giving the effect of a wreath of Christmas greenery. Then stick a toothpick into each vegetable, securing these to the ring, filling in the gaps. Arrange vegetables so that they give a multicolored effect. If desired, serve with a dip off to the side (instead of in the middle, to retain the wreath effect). Serves 10 - 12 or more.

Red and Green Salad
with Vinaigrette Dressing

1 bunch romaine and/or green leaf lettuce
1 head red leaf lettuce
1 bunch radishes, optional
Dressing:
1 clove garlic
1 tsp. sugar
1/2 tsp. salt
Ground pepper
3 Tbsp. salad oil
1 Tbsp. vinegar

Wash both kinds of lettuce, and drain thoroughly; gently break into bite-sized pieces. Wash radishes, remove ends, and cut into thin slices. Mix lettuce and radishes in a pretty salad bowl, and refrigerate. In a small jar, cut the clove of garlic into several small pieces or put it through a garlic press (for stronger garlic flavor). Add sugar, salt, ground pepper (to taste), salad oil, and vinegar. Shake all ingredients vigorously. If garlic was cut up, remove from dressing mixture before pouring over salad. Toss gently with dressing, and serve immediately. Serves 8 or more.

Ceasar Salad
3 cloves garlic
2 Tbsp. anchovy paste, optional
1 tsp. Worcestershire sauce
1/2 cup olive oil
Freshly ground pepper
2 Tbsp. wine vinegar
1 head romaine lettuce, broken into pieces
1 egg, boiled 1 minute
1 cup croutons
1/2 cup grated Parmesan cheese (fresh is best)

In a wooden bowl mash garlic, anchovy paste, Worcestershire sauce, 1 tablespoon olive oil, and pepper. Place in refrigerator until you're ready to make the salad. Add remaining olive oil and vinegar, and blend well. Toss dressing with romaine. Break egg into salad and toss again. Add croutons and toss. Add cheese to taste. Serves 6 to 8.

Vegetables

Baked Beans
2 cans (31 oz. each) pork and beans
1 Tbsp. prepared mustard
1/2 cup ketchup
1 tsp. Worcestershire sauce
2 Tbsp. brown sugar
1/4 cup chopped onion
Bacon strips, if desired

Drain pork and beans in a strainer or colander. Mix beans and all remaining ingredients except bacon together thoroughly. Pour into a large greased baking dish or casserole. Place strips of bacon across top of beans, if desired. Bake at 400° for one hour or longer. Makes 8 or more servings.

Twice-baked Potatoes
4 medium-large baking potatoes (not red potatoes)
1 stick butter or margarine
Hot milk, to moisten
Sour cream, optional
Salt and pepper, to taste
2 - 4 Tbsp. chopped green onions and/or crumbled crisp bacon, optional
Grated cheddar cheese, optional

Scrub potato skins with a brush and water. Bake potatoes at 425° for 60 to 80 minutes, depending on their size, until fork-tender. Take an oval-shaped slice from the top of each. Scoop out almost all of the potato; mash. Add butter, enough hot milk to make potatoes very moist, and/or sour cream. Add salt and pepper to taste. Beat until smooth and fluffy. If you are using additional ingredients, fill potato shells 1/2 full with mashed potatoes, then divide green onions and/or crumbled bacon evenly among shells. Pile remaining mashed potatoes atop. Sprinkle with grated cheddar cheese, if desired. Return to oven at 375° for 12 to 15 minutes or until hot and lightly browned. Serves 4.

Broccoli with Lemon and Red Pepper Flakes

2 bunches of fresh broccoli, about 1 1/2 - 2 pounds each
Juice of 1 fresh lemon
Dried red pepper flakes, to taste
Salt, to taste
1/4 cup extra virgin olive oil

Wash and trim the broccoli, peel the stems, and cut into thin slices. Cut the flowerets into 2-inch pieces and reserve them. In a large steamer set over boiling water, steam the broccoli stems, covered, for 5 minutes, or until they are crisp-tender, and transfer them to a bowl. In the steamer steam the reserved flowerets, covered, for 3 to 5 minutes, or until they are crisp-tender. Transfer them to a separate bowl. Sprinkle the stems and the flowerets with the lemon juice, red pepper flakes, and salt to taste. Drizzle the olive oil over them, and toss each mixture well. Arrange the stems and also the flowerets creatively on a platter. Serves 8.

Baked Squash Medley

4 medium summer or yellow squash
2 slices bacon
1 medium tomato
1/4 cup chopped green pepper
1/2 cup chopped onion
1 cup grated cheese
1 tsp. salt
1/4 tsp. pepper
1/2 cup dry bread crumbs
1/4 cup melted butter or margarine

Boil squash for 6 to 8 minutes. Cut squash in half lengthwise; scoop out seeds and discard. Fry bacon until crisp; crumble and combine with tomato, green pepper, onion, cheese, salt, and pepper. Spoon mixture into squash. Top with mixture of bread crumbs and butter or margarine. Bake at 350° for 30 minutes. Serves 8.

Tomato Stack-Ups

3 large tomatoes, ripe but firm
1 cup shredded Swiss or other cheese
1 (10 oz.) package frozen chopped broccoli
1/4 cup chopped onion

Cook broccoli according to package directions, and drain throughly. Cut tomatoes into 1/2" slices. Set aside 2 tablespoons of the shredded cheese. Combine remaining cheese, broccoli, and chopped onion. Place tomato slices on a greased baking sheet. Spoon broccoli mixture onto tomatoes. Sprinkle with reserved cheese. Broil 7 to 8 inches from the heat until cheese is bubbly and golden brown, approximately 10 to 12 minutes. Serves 6 to 8.

Missy Potatoes

1 (2 pound) package frozen hash browns, thawed
1 (16 oz.) carton sour cream
1 can cream of celery or cream of mushroom soup, undiluted
1 cup shredded sharp cheddar cheese
1/2 cup butter or margarine, softened
1 tsp. salt
1 tsp. pepper
1/2 cup buttery cracker crumbs (like Ritz)

Combine all ingredients except cracker crumbs. Spoon into a greased 13 x 9 x 2" baking dish. Sprinkle cracker crumbs evenly over top of potato mixture. Bake at 350° for 40 minutes, or until bubbly.

Veggie Tree
2 - 4 cups of your favorite dip
Celery strips, cut in uniform lengths
Carrot curls or short strips
Cauliflower flowerets
Green pepper slices
Cherry tomatoes
Broccoli flowerets
Small radishes
Zucchini or cucumber slices, cut thin

Prepare or purchase 2 cups (per veggie tree) of your favorite dip, preferably one that is white in color. Instead of serving it in a bowl, spread it approximately 1/2" thick over a baking sheet, all the way to the edges. Wash and cut up all of the vegetables. Make the outline of a Christmas tree, as large as possible on the sheet, with the uniform-sized celery strips. Then "decorate" the tree with a variety of multicolored veggies! Surround the sheet with additional bowls of vegetables for dipping. Each "veggie tree" will serve 12 to 15.

Orange Glazed Sweet Potatoes
6 medium sweet potatoes
1/3 cup frozen orange juice concentrate
1/2 cup brown sugar
1/2 cup butter or margarine, melted
1 tsp. salt

Cook sweet potatoes in jackets, covered in boiling water approximately 30 - 40 minutes, until almost fork-tender. Combine remaining ingredients to make glaze. Peel cooked potatoes, slice, and put in a baking dish. Pour glaze over potatoes, and bake at 350° for 20 to 30 minutes. Serves 6 to 8.

Side Dishes and Extras

Risengrøt (Rice Porridge)
2 Tbsp. butter
1 1/4 cups long-cooking rice
6 cups whole milk
1 egg, beaten
Cinnamon
Sugar
A few almonds

Melt butter in a heavy saucepan. Rinse rice in cold water first, then in hot water 3 times. Stir rice into melted butter. Add milk, and place over lowest heat. Stir occasionally, and let this mixture simmer for about 1 1/2 hours. Add more milk only if necessary. Mixture should be velvety and smooth. Add salt, to taste, and stir in beaten egg. (It is best to stir a little of the porridge into the egg in a separate bowl, then add egg mixture to porridge.) Pour into soup plates, place a lump of butter in the center of each, and sprinkle with cinnamon and sugar. If desired, bury an almond in one or more servings, to determine who receives a prize! Serve with milk or red fruit juice. If there are any leftovers, let cool, add whipped cream, and top with your favorite jam, to serve as a dessert. Serves 4 or more.

Lefse (Potato Crepe)

4 1/2 cups instant mashed potatoes
4 cups boiling water
1 stick margarine or butter
1 1/2 tsp. salt
1 1/2 Tbsp. sugar
1 1/2 cups flour

Cook potatoes according to package directions, but using the first five ingredients. Chill until entire mixture is cold to the touch. Mix 1 1/2 cups of flour with 3 cups of the mixture. Dust work surface with a little flour to prevent sticking. Roll the potato mixture dough into a log. Cut segments off, and roll out into large thin pancakes, using a rolling pin. These should be about the size of a tortilla. Fry on a hot ungreased griddle, flipping them at least once, until the pancakes are thoroughly cooked and light golden brown. Cool. Serve with butter, sugar, and cinnamon, or with butter and goat cheese. Roll up pancakes to eat.

Cornbread Dressing

1 cup chopped onion
2 cups diced celery
1/2 cup (1 stick) margarine or butter
2 quarts bread cubes from 2 - 4-day-old bread
2 quarts cornbread cubes
1 - 2 Tbsp. salt
1/2 tsp. pepper
1 Tbsp. poultry seasoning
4 eggs, beaten
4 - 6 cups hot broth or water
4 hard-cooked eggs, chopped

Cook onion and celery in margarine or butter on low heat until onion is soft but not browned. Meanwhile, blend bread cubes, cornbread cubes, and seasonings. Add onion, celery, margarine or butter, and beaten eggs, and stir. Add broth gradually, stirring gently. Add hard-cooked eggs and more seasonings, if desired. Bake in a large baking pan or casserole during the last hour that your turkey is roasting. Serves 12 or more.

Giblet Gravy

1/4 cup plus 2 Tbsp. turkey drippings
1/4 cup plus 2 Tbsp. flour
4 cups turkey broth, milk, or water
Cooked giblet meat from turkey
2 hard-cooked eggs
Salt and pepper, to taste

Blend drippings and flour, stirring constantly. Add cool liquid all at once. Cook, stirring constantly, until thickened. Simmer about 5 minutes. Add salt and pepper to taste. Add cooked, cut-up giblet meat and diced eggs to gravy, and heat thoroughly. Makes 6 cups.

Spicy Fruit Compote

1 can (17 oz.) apricot halves
1 can (16 oz.) peach slices
1 can (16 oz.) pitted purple plums or pitted dark
  cherries
1 can (16 oz.) pineapple chunks
1 can (16 oz.) spiced apple rings, optional
1/2 cup orange juice
1/4 - 1/2 cup brown sugar
2 Tbsp. melted butter or margarine

1/2 cup coconut
1 tsp. cinnamon
1/2 tsp. each of nutmeg and ginger

Drain all canned fruits well. Cut apricot halves and peach slices into halves. Cut plums and apple rings into fourths. Place all fruits in a large baking pan. Mix orange juice, brown sugar, melted butter or margarine, coconut, and spices together. Pour this mixture over fruit. Bake at 425° for approximately 15 - 20 minutes, or until thoroughly heated. Serve warm, not hot. Serves 8 - 10 or more.

Cranberry Bread

2 cups sifted flour
1 cup sugar
1 1/2 tsp. baking powder
1/2 tsp. baking soda
1 tsp. salt
1/3 - 3/4 cup orange juice
1/2 tsp. orange rind, optional
2 Tbsp. melted butter or margarine
1 egg, well beaten
1/2 - 1 cup chopped nuts
2 cups fresh cranberries, chopped or cut in halves

Preheat oven to 350°. Sift together flour, sugar, baking powder, baking soda, and salt. Use 3/4 cup orange juice, or add enough water to orange juice to make 3/4 cup. Combine orange juice, orange rind, melted butter, and beaten egg. Pour this mixture into the dry ingredients, mixing just enough to dampen. Fold in cranberries and chopped nuts, blending gently but thoroughly. Spoon into a greased 9 x 5 x 3" loaf pan, spreading it evenly, making corners and

sides slightly higher than center. Bake at 350° for 65 minutes. Remove from pan after 20 minutes and cool on wire rack. Makes 1 loaf.

Zucchini Nut Bread

2 cups sugar
1 cup vegetable oil
3 eggs
1 Tbsp. ground cinnamon
1 tsp. baking powder
1 tsp. baking soda
1 tsp. vanilla
1/2 tsp. ground ginger
1/2 tsp. salt
3 1/4 cups sifted flour
3 cups shredded, unpeeled zucchini (about 3 medium zucchini)
1 cup chopped nuts

Preheat oven to 325°. Combine all the ingredients except the flour, zucchini, and nuts in the large bowl of an electric mixer. Beat for about 2 minutes, scraping sides of bowl often, until thoroughly blended. Remove bowl from mixer. Fold in the flour with a spatula until blended, then fold in the zucchini and the nuts. Divide the mixture evenly among the greased pans: two 8 x 4" loaves or six 5 x 3" loaves. Bake on center rack at 325° about 75 minutes for the large loaves, and 60 minutes for the small loaves, or until toothpick inserted in the center comes out clean. Cool for approximately 10 to 15 minutes, then turn loaves out onto a wire rack to cool completely. Serve the bread warm with whipped cream cheese, if desired.

Pumpkin Bread

3 cups sugar
1 cup salad oil
3 eggs
2 cups canned pumpkin
3 cups flour
1/2 tsp. salt
1/2 tsp. baking powder
1 tsp. baking soda
1 tsp. ground cloves
1 tsp. cinnamon
1 tsp. nutmeg

Preheat oven to 350°. Mix first 4 ingredients, then add sifted flour, salt, baking powder and soda, and spices. Bake at 350° in greased and floured pans: 1 bundt pan for about 50 - 55 minutes, or 3 (1 pound each) coffee cans, also greased and floured, filled 1/2 full, for 1 hour or longer. Check for doneness with a cake tester or toothpick. Cool for approximately 20 minutes, then turn loaves out onto a wire rack to cool completely. Freezes well.

Scottish Scones

1 1/2 cups flour
1/4 cup sugar
1 Tbsp. baking powder
1/2 tsp. salt
3/4 cup butter or margarine
1 1/2 cups oats
1/3 cup chopped pecans, optional
1/3 cup milk

Sift together flour, sugar, baking powder, and salt. Cut butter into dry ingredients. Stir in oats and chopped pecans. Add milk; stir until just moistened. Roll out dough on floured board into a circle 1/2 inch thick. Cut circle into small pie-shaped wedges. Bake at 425° for 12 to 15 minutes, or until lightly golden. Serve with butter or a glaze made of 2 Tbsp. softened butter and 1/4 cup honey blended together. Spread on scones while they are still hot. Makes 6 to 8 servings.

Pumpkin Apple Streusel Muffins

2 1/2 cups flour
2 cups sugar
1 Tbsp. pumpkin pie spice
1 tsp. baking soda
1/2 tsp. salt
2 eggs, beaten
1 cup solid pack pumpkin
1/2 cup vegetable oil
2 cups peeled, chopped apple
1/2 cup chopped nuts
1/2 cup raisins

Streusel Topping
2 Tbsp. flour
1/4 cup sugar
1/2 tsp. cinnamon
1/4 cup (1/2 stick) butter or margarine

In a large bowl combine the first 5 ingredients; set aside. In a medium bowl combine beaten eggs, pumpkin, and oil. Add liquid ingredients to dry ingredients; stir just until moistened. Stir in apples, nuts, and raisins. Spoon batter into greased or paper muffin cups. Fill almost to top. For Streusel Topping, blend flour, sugar, and cinnamon together in a small bowl. Cut in 1/4 cup cold butter or margarine until mixture is crumbly. Sprinkle topping over batter. Bake at 400° for 20 minutes or longer, until toothpick comes out clean.

Desserts

Chocolate Crinkles

1/2 cup butter
1 2/3 cup sugar
2 eggs
2 squares (1 oz. each) chocolate, melted or 4 Tbsp. cocoa
2 cups flour
2 tsp. baking powder
1/2 tsp. salt
1/3 cup milk
2 tsp. vanilla

Cream together butter and sugar, add eggs. Add remaining ingredients, and mix thoroughly. Cover dough tightly and refrigerate overnight. With dough firm, and powdered sugar on your hands, roll dough in 1 - 1 1/2" balls and then in powdered sugar. Place on a greased cookie sheet. Bake at 350° for 14 - 15 minutes. Cookies should still be soft, not crisp. Store in airtight container to keep moist and chewy. Makes about 4 dozen.

Sand Tarts

1 cup butter (gives best flavor)
1/4 cup powdered sugar
1 Tbsp. water
1 Tbsp. vanilla
2 cups flour
1 cup finely chopped pecans
Additional powdered sugar

Blend first 6 ingredients together in order listed. Chill dough slightly, then make into 2 rolls and chill thoroughly, overnight if possible. Cut in slices while dough is cold. Bake on ungreased cookie sheet at 300° for 20 minutes. Immediately after removing from oven, sift powdered sugar over cookies (this is the additional amount). Let cool on cookie sheet, then use waxed paper between layers for storing. Makes about 3 dozen.

Red and Green Sugar Cookies

1 cup (2 sticks) margarine
2 cups sugar
2 eggs
1 tsp. vanilla
3 cups flour
1 tsp. cream of tartar
1 tsp. baking soda
1 tsp. salt

Cream margarine and sugar; beat in eggs one at a time. Add vanilla. Sift dry ingredients together and blend into creamed mixture. Chill several hours or overnight, and keep dough chilled while forming in 1 - 1 1/2" balls. Dip the tops of the balls in green or red sugar just before baking, then place sugar-side-up on well-greased cookie sheet. Bake at 350° for about 12 minutes, or until they swell and then shrink slightly. Let cool on the sheet about 1 minute; they get too crisp and break if allowed to cool too long. If cookies seem hard to remove, place

177

them back in the oven for several seconds. For ease, make one entire sheet using red sugar, then one using green sugar. Makes about 6 dozen cookies.

Mini Cherry Cheesecakes

1 package (8 oz.) cream cheese, softened
1 can (15 oz.) sweetened condensed milk
1/3 cup lemon juice
1/2 cup sour cream
18 vanilla wafers
18 muffin papers
1 can cherry pie filling (or fresh fruit)
Whipped cream, optional

Place cream cheese in a bowl and cream until soft and smooth. Combine sweetened condensed milk and lemon juice. Gradually add to cream cheese. Fold in the sour cream. Place muffin papers in muffin tins. Place 1 vanilla wafer in the bottom of each muffin paper. Spoon creamy mixture over each vanilla wafer, until about 2/3 full. Refrigerate. To serve, garnish with 1 - 2 tablespoons of cherry pie filling (or a piece of fresh fruit). Add a dollop of whipped cream, if desired. Makes 18 servings.

Date Pudding Cake with Butter Sauce

1 cup dates, each cut in about 6 pieces
1 cup boiling water
1/3 cup butter or margarine
1 cup sugar
1 egg
1 cup flour
1 tsp. baking soda
1/2 tsp. salt
1 cup chopped pecans
Butter Sauce
1 1/2 cups sugar
1/2 cup half-and-half
1 stick butter or margarine

Pour boiling water over date pieces and let stand. Cream together butter and sugar; add egg. Blend in dates and water. Add flour, baking soda, and salt, then chopped pecans. Blend thoroughly. Bake at 325° in 8 1/2 x 12" pan for 30 minutes, or until toothpick comes out clean. Cool. For sauce, blend together sugar, half-and-half, and butter. Cook in a double boiler, if available, or on extremely low heat for 2 - 3 hours, stirring occasionally with an egg beater. Pour sauce over warm pudding cake and top with whipped cream or whipped topping if desired. Serves 12 or more.

Peppermint Fondue

1 stick butter or margarine, softened
2 boxes (16 oz. each) powdered sugar, sifted
2 egg whites
1/4 tsp. salt
1/2 cup or more light cream or half-and-half
1 tsp. vanilla
4 - 6 ounces peppermint candies or sticks, crushed

Blend softened butter in a large mixing bowl with powdered sugar. Add egg whites and salt. Beat well. Add cream and beat until fluffy. Add vanilla and beat again. Unwrap and place peppermint candies or sticks inside a heavy-duty plastic freezer bag. Wrap newspapers or an old towel around bag, and use a hammer (on a cement floor) to crush the candies almost to powder. (Children love this job, but supervise them please!) Blend into creamed mixture. This will thin out as it heats up. Place in fondue pot, stirring constantly until mixture is hot. Reduce to low heat, still stirring frequently to prevent sticking. Spear bite-sized cubes of brownies, pound cake, and pieces of fruit on fondue forks. Twirl in fondue, drain, and cool momentarily. Serves 8 or more.

Chocolate Fondue

2 Tbsp. light corn syrup
3/4 cup (or more) half-and-half or light cream
2 bars (5 oz. each) milk chocolate, broken into small pieces
1/4 cup toasted almonds or chopped pecans, optional
1 tsp. vanilla

Blend corn syrup and half-and-half in saucepan on high heat, stirring constantly. Lower heat; stir in chocolate pieces. Heat, stirring constantly, until chocolate is melted. Add nuts and vanilla. Pour into fondue pot, and keep on low heat. Stir frequently. Spear pieces of fresh fruit, such as apple slices, strawberries, banana slices, pineapple, etc., and cubes of pound cake (cut about 2 hours early, to dry out a little) and dip in chocolate fondue. Stir these in a figure-eight motion. If desired, roll dipped fruit or cake in more chopped nuts or coconut. Serves 4 - 6.

Fresh Apple Cake

1/2 cup shortening
1 1/2 cup sugar
2 beaten eggs
1/4 tsp. salt
1/2 tsp. nutmeg
1/2 tsp. cinnamon
1 tsp. vanilla
3 - 4 cups chopped raw apples
1/2 cup chopped pecans
1 1/2 cups flour
1 tsp. baking soda

Cream shortening and sugar. Add beaten eggs, salt, spices, and vanilla. Add chopped apples and chopped nuts. Sift together flour and baking soda, and add to first mixture. Pour into a greased and floured 13 x 9 x 2" baking pan, and bake at 350° for 35 - 40 minutes, or until a toothpick comes out clean. Serve with a dollop of whipped cream. Or if desired, frost with Butter Cream Icing. Serves 15 or more.

Butter Cream Icing

1/2 stick soft butter or margarine
1 box (16 oz.) sifted powdered sugar
1 egg white, optional
1/4 tsp salt
3 Tbsp. half-and-half or whole milk
1 tsp. vanilla

Cream butter or margarine with electric mixer, sift powdered sugar into bowl, and blend thoroughly. Add egg white and salt. Beat well. Add half-and-half; beat until fluffy. Add vanilla last, and beat thoroughly. Enough to ice a 13 x 9 x 2" cake.

Frosting Mortar for Gingerbread House

4 egg whites
4 tsp. water
1/4 tsp. cream of tartar
6 cups powdered sugar

Place egg whites, water, and cream of tartar in large mixer bowl, and beat until just foamy. Keep beating as you add the powdered sugar 1 cup at a time. Keep beating at high speed until frosting mortar is very stable and white. For colored mortar, add a few drops of food coloring or a very small dab of paste color, increasing the amount until the desired color is achieved. Makes enough mortar for 3 - 4 gingerbread houses.

Hot Fudge Sauce

2 cups sugar
2/3 cup cocoa
1/4 cup plus 2 Tbsp. flour
1 tsp. salt
2 cups whole milk
2 Tbsp. butter or margarine
2 tsp. vanilla

In a medium saucepan thoroughly blend sugar, cocoa, flour, and salt. Add milk. Cook over medium heat until thickened. Remove from heat and add butter, vanilla, and any other extract (mint, etc.) desired. Serve hot or cold, refrigerating remainder. Makes approximately 3 cups.

Brownie Sundaes

1 recipe brownies, homemade or bakery-type
1/2 gallon vanilla or peppermint ice cream
Hot Fudge Sauce (see previous recipe)
Chopped nuts or other toppings

Place one brownie on each serving plate. Put 1 - 2 scoops of ice cream on top. Heat Hot Fudge Sauce, and pour or spoon it over ice cream. Top with chopped nuts, colored candy sprinkles, crushed peppermint candy, etc. This recipe is great for a

crowd, and also for unexpected company, because you can keep all the ingredients on hand and in the freezer. It is also quick to assemble. Serves 15 or more.

Cherry Delight

1 1/2 cups flour
1 1/2 sticks margarine, softened
2 Tbsp. sugar
1 cup pecans, chopped
2 cups sifted powdered sugar
1 package (8 oz.) cream cheese, softened
1 tsp. vanilla
1 small package Dream Whip
1 can cherry pie filling

Mix together flour, margarine, sugar, and chopped pecans. Press into a 13 x 9 x 2" baking pan, with floured fingers to prevent sticking. Bake at 350° for 20 minutes; crust should be lightly golden brown. Blend together powdered sugar, cream cheese, and vanilla. Set aside. In another bowl, mix Dream Whip according to package directions. Add Dream Whip to cream cheese mixture, and fold in gently. Pour over cooled crust. Carefully pour can of cherry pie filling over top evenly. Refrigerate until serving. Because this dessert is rich, it can be cut in up to 24 pieces.

Fresh Banana Cake

2/3 cup margarine, softened
2 1/2 cups sifted flour
1 2/3 cups sugar
1 1/4 tsp. baking powder
1 tsp. baking soda

1/2 tsp. salt
1 1/4 cups mashed ripe banana
2/3 cup buttermilk or soured milk
2 eggs
1 tsp. vanilla
3/4 cup chopped pecans or English walnuts

In a large mixing bowl, allow margarine to soften. Sift in all dry ingredients. Add mashed banana and blend thoroughly. (If using soured milk, add a scant tablespoon vinegar to 2/3 cup whole milk, stir, and let sit for several minutes.) Add half the buttermilk or soured milk, and blend until all flour is dampened. Beat on medium-high speed 2 minutes. Add remaining buttermilk or soured milk, eggs, and vanilla; beat 2 minutes longer. Fold in chopped nuts. Bake at 350° in a greased and floured 13 x 9 x 2" for approximately 45 minutes. Or if you're using 2 (9") round cake pans, bake for approximately 35 minutes, or until toothpick comes out clean from either. Cool 10 minutes in round pans before removing; place on wire rack and cool again thoroughly. Fill and frost round layers, or frost top of oblong cake, with Butter Cream Icing (see recipe in this section). Serves 12 - 15 or more.

Lemon Meringue Pie

1 (9") baked pie shell
1 1/2 cups sugar
1/3 cup plus 1 Tbsp. cornstarch
3 egg yolks, slightly beaten
1 1/2 cups water
3 Tbsp. butter or margarine
1/2 - 1 tsp. grated lemon peel

1/2 cup lemon juice
2 drops yellow food color, if desired
Meringue for pie:
3 egg whites
1/4 tsp. cream of tartar
1/4 cup plus 2 Tbsp. sugar
1/2 tsp. vanilla

Bake pie shell. Adjust oven to 400°. Stir together sugar and cornstarch in a medium saucepan. Blend egg yolks and water; gradually stir into sugar mixture. Cook over medium heat, stirring constantly until mixture thickens and boils. Stir and boil gently 1 minute. Remove from heat, stir in butter, lemon peel, lemon juice, and food color. Immediately pour into baked pie shell. For meringue: beat egg whites and cream of tartar until foamy. Beat in sugar, 1 tablespoon at a time; continue beating until stiff and glossy. Do not underbeat. Add and blend in vanilla. Heap meringue onto hot pie filling; spread over filling, carefully sealing meringue to edges of crust to prevent shrinking. Bake about 10 minutes or until meringue is a delicate golden color. Cool away from drafts. Serves 8 - 10.

Frosty Pumpkin Pie

1 cup canned pumpkin
1/2 cup brown sugar
1/8 tsp. salt
1 tsp. cinnamon
1/8 tsp. ground cloves
1/4 tsp. nutmeg
1 quart vanilla ice cream, softened
1 (9") graham cracker crust

Combine pumpkin, sugar, salt, and spices; blend together. Add softened ice cream; mix until well blended. Pour into graham cracker crust. Freeze until firm. Serves 8 or more.

Pecan Pie

3 eggs
3/4 cup sugar
1/2 tsp. vanilla
1 cup corn syrup
1/2 stick margarine, melted
1/4 tsp. salt
1 cup pecans, pieces or halves
1 unbaked 9" pie crust

Beat together eggs, sugar, vanilla, corn syrup, melted margarine, and salt. Chop pecans into large pieces or use halves (halves make the pie a little harder to cut, but they look pretty!). Place pecans in the bottom of an unbaked pie crust, and gently pour the liquid mixture over the pecans. Bake at 325° for 60 - 75 minutes, or until center of pie is almost firm. If the crust is getting too brown near the end, place a flat sheet of foil over the top to finish baking. Cool. Serves 8 or more.

Christmas Tree Cake

1 white or yellow cake mix
2 recipes Butter Cream Icing (see this section)
Green food color or paste color
Candy decorations, a variety

Bake cake mix, according to package directions, in a 13 x 9 x 2" baking pan. Cool for approximately 15 - 20 minutes in pan, then remove and place on a cutting board. Cool thoroughly. Cut a 2" wide strip off one of the 9" sides of the cake, and set this aside. Cut remaining rectangle diagonally lengthwise. On a large serving platter (or board covered with foil), place the two triangles directly next to each other to form one big triangle; the cut sides will be the 2 outside edges of the "tree." Cut the 2" strip in half, and use one half as the "trunk." (Eat other half!) Tint both recipes of icing your desired shade of green by adding several drops of food color at a time or a very small amount of paste color. Blend thoroughly. Ice entire "tree" with green icing. Decorate with colorful gum drops, jelly beans, red or black pieces of licorice, silver candy balls, M&M's, red hots, and so on. Serves 12 - 15 or more.

Pistachio Pudding Dessert

1 cup flour
1 stick margarine, melted or softened
1 cup chopped pecans or English walnuts
1 package (8 oz.) cream cheese, softened
3/4 cup powdered sugar
1 medium or large carton Cool Whip
2 small packages (3 1/2 or 4 oz. each) instant pista-
 chio pudding
3 cups whole milk

Mix together flour, margarine, and chopped nuts. Press into a 13 x 9 x 2" baking pan. Bake in a preheated 350° oven for 15 minutes. Cool completely. Blend together cream cheese, powdered sugar, and 1 cup of Cool Whip. Spread onto cooled crust. Mix together instant pudding and 3 cups milk; blend or shake until thick. Pour over cream cheese layer. Top with remainder of Cool Whip. Refrigerate until ready to serve. Makes up to 18 - 24 servings, as it is very rich. Refrigerate leftovers.

Beverages

Frosted Strawberry Punch
2 packages (.14 oz. each) strawberry Kool-Aid
1 large can (46 oz.) unsweetened pineapple juice
Scant 1 1/2 cups sugar
1 Tbsp. lemon juice
1 quart water
1 quart or 1 liter lemon-lime soda or ginger ale

Have clean disposable gallon milk jugs available—one per recipe of punch. Mix together all ingredients except lemon-lime soda or ginger ale. Pour into jugs and freeze until solid. About 5 hours ahead of serving, take out of the freezer and let thaw at room temperature. Punch should be slushy, with lots of ice left in it. You may need to cut the top off the jug to pour into punch bowl. Add lemon-lime soda or ginger ale just as punch is to be served. Makes about 1 gallon. Note: Besides using red Kool-Aid for Christmas (or Valentine's Day), you can make the punch using yellow or pink Kool-Aid for Easter, green Kool-Aid for St. Patrick's Day, etc. A versatile punch!

Golden Wassail
4 cups unsweetened pineapple juice
1 can (11 1/2oz.) apricot nectar
4 cups apple cider
1 cup orange juice
4 inches stick cinnamon

1/2 -1 tsp. whole cloves
1/4 tsp. salt
1/4 tsp. ground cardamom

Pour juices into pot of a 1-gallon (or larger) drip coffeemaker. Place remaining ingredients in basket of coffeemaker. Allow to go through cycle. If your coffeemaker holds less than one gallon, use a 4-quart or larger saucepan, simmer 15 - 20 minutes, and remove cinnamon stick and cloves from pan after simmering. Serve piping hot. Makes 20 (1/2-cup) servings.

Easy Hot Spiced Cider
1/2 gallon apple cider
1/2 tsp. allspice
1/2 tsp. cinnamon
1/2 tsp. whole cloves
1 stick cinnamon
Scant 1/4 cup brown sugar
Scant 1/4 cup granulated sugar

Mix all ingredients together in a 3-quart (or larger) saucepan. Simmer for 30 minutes. Makes 1/2 gallon.

Frozen Strawberry (or Raspberry) Glacés
8 pints fresh strawberries (or raspberries)
4 cups superfine sugar, or to taste
2 quarts cold ginger ale

Thoroughly wash and hull strawberries or raspberries. Whirl berries, a quart at a time, in a blender until smooth, about 1 minute. Sweeten to taste with approximately 4 cups sugar. Freeze firm in ice cube trays. Just before serving, remove from trays, and put in blender again, adding cold ginger ale a little at a time. Blend on low speed for 10 seconds. Serve at once in chilled punch bowl. Makes approximately 64 (1/2-cup) servings.

Strawberry Blondes

4 cups cold milk
4 cups orange juice, chilled
4 packages (10 oz. each) frozen strawberries, partially thawed
8 scoops vanilla ice cream
Whipped cream
Red food color

Blend milk, orange juice, strawberries, and vanilla ice cream together on high speed in a blender until thoroughly mixed. Blend a drop or two of red food color with whipped cream to tint pink. Pour liquid into chilled glasses and garnish with a puff of pink whipped cream. Serves 8.

Banana Punch

1 can (46 oz.) pineapple juice
2 cans (12 oz. each) frozen orange juice
1 can (12 oz.) frozen lemonade
5 ripe bananas, put through blender
2 cups sugar
6 cups water
7 bottles (28 oz. each) ginger ale or 6 - 7 bottles (32 oz. each) 7-Up

Mix first 6 ingredients together thoroughly and freeze in clean gallon milk jugs. Let thaw for several hours before serving. Blend in ginger ale or 7-Up as you're ready to serve. Makes 50 or more (1/2-cup) servings.

Tip Your Hat Punch

1 can (6 oz.) frozen orange juice
1 can (6 oz.) frozen pineapple juice
2 cups cranberry juice
Red food color
1 bottle (32 oz.) ginger ale, chilled
1 pint pineapple sherbet

In punch bowl, reconstitute orange and pineapple juices according to directions on cans. Add cranberry juice and enough red food color to obtain a deeper red. Just before serving, add chilled ginger ale. Float scoops of pineapple sherbet on top. Makes 25 (1/2-cup) servings.

Hot Spicy Pineapple Punch

1 can (46 oz.) pineapple juice
1 cup cranberry juice
1/2 cup brown or granulated sugar
2 Tbsp. butter or margarine
1/2 tsp. cinnamon
1/4 tsp. nutmeg
1/8 tsp. ground cloves
Lemon slices
Whole cloves

Combine first seven ingredients in a 3-quart or larger saucepan. Bring to a gentle boil; reduce heat. Simmer for 15 minutes. Serve in punch cups or mugs. Press a clove into a lemon slice to float on top of each cup of punch. Makes 12 (1/2-cup) servings.

Frosted Cranberry Snow

3 cups cranberry or raspberry sparkler
2 large cans (12 oz. each) frozen lemonade

4 lemonade cans of cranberry cocktail juice
2 lemonade cans of chilled 7-Up

Mix together fruit sparkler, lemonade, and cranberry juice, and freeze until firm. When ready to serve, mix in blender, slowly adding chilled 7-Up. Blend until just icy. Pour into chilled glasses with stems. Serves 10 - 12.

....

Resources

Albright, Barbara. "The Great Cookie Party." *Family Fun Magazine*, November, 1993, pp. 102 – 108.

Better Homes and Gardens Books. *The Better Homes and Gardens New Cookbook*. Des Moines, Iowa: Meredith Corporation Book Group, 1989.

Book of Christmas Decorations. Tokyo, Japan: Ondorisha Publishers, 1988.

Brokaw, Meredith, and Gilbar, Annie. *The Penny Whistle Christmas Party Book*. New York: Simon and Schuster, 1991.

"Christmas Dinner." *Gourmet—The Magazine of Good Living*, December 1992, pp. 148 - 156.

Christmas Ornaments. Des Moines, Iowa: Meredith Corporation Book Group, 1991.

Clegg, Holly Berkowitz. *From a Louisiana Kitchen*. Baton Rouge: Holly B. Clegg Publishers, 1993.

Craig, Katherine, and Cook, Deanna F. "A Family Tree-Trimming Party." *Family Fun Magazine*, November, 1993, pp. 84 - 94.

DuNah, Delores M., and Groudle, H. Jean. *The Non-Alcoholic Drink Book*. Old Tappan, New Jersey: Fleming H. Revell, 1971.

The Evolution of Cajun and Creole Cuisine. Donaldsonville, Louisiana: Chef John D. Folse and Company, 1990.

Faber, Kristie, ed. *Images*, 3 vols. Wichita, Kansas: The Pioneer Balloon Company, November/December 1991, 1992, 1993.

A Family Christmas. Pleasantville, New York: The Reader's Digest Association, 1984.

Junior League of New Orleans. *Jambalaya*. New Orleans, Louisiana: Hard Graphics, 1983.

Junior League of The City of Washington, Inc. *Think Christmas*. Washington, D.C.: McArdie, 1975.

Maltin, Leonard. *Movie and Video Guide*. New York: Penguin Group, 1993.

Okrent, Rebecca Lazear. "House-to-House Party." *Family Fun Magazine*, November 1993, pp. 79 - 86, 199.

Philharmonic League of Kansas City, Missouri. *Finger Foods*. Kansas City: Smith-Grieves, 1978.

Spirit of Christmas: *Creative Holiday Ideas*, 3 vols. North Little Rock, Arkansas: Leisure Arts, Inc., 1987 - 1989.

Sprague, Marty. *Menus and Meals—In Minutes!* Irvine, California: Palmer Publishers, 1989.

Stewart, Shelley, and Voce, Jo. *Decorating Craft Ideas for Christmas 1984*. Birmingham, Alabama: Oxmoor House, Inc., 1984.

Texas Electric Service Company. *Energy Aware Holiday Fare.* Fort Worth, Texas, n. d.

_____. *Favorite Southwest Recipes.* Fort Worth, Texas, n. d.

_____. *Heritage Holiday Recipes.* Fort Worth, Texas, n. d.

_____. *Southwest Recipes: The Best of Twenty-Five Years.* Fort Worth, n. d.

Wright, Linda Baltzell, comp. and ed. *Christmas Is Coming,* 3 vols. Birmingham, Alabama: Oxmoor House, Inc., 1991 - 1993.